THE MICHIGAN THEATER

ANN ARBOR'S HOME *for*

FINE FILM *and*

the PERFORMING ARTS

SINCE 1928

by Henry B. Aldridge

with Russell B. Collins

2013

The Michigan Theater: Ann Arbor's Home for Fine Film and the Performing Arts Since 1928

Books may be purchased by contacting the Michigan Theater Foundation
603 East Liberty Street, Ann Arbor, Michigan 48104
734-668-8397 or at michtheater.org.

Cover and book design by:
Marty Somberg / Somberg Design / www.sombergdesign.com

Editor: Domenica Trevor

Index: Alexa Selph

Proofreaders: Bob Land and Domenica Trevor

Book Consultant: Alexa Selph

Publisher: Michigan Theater Foundation, 603 East Liberty Street, Ann Arbor, Michigan 48104.

Hardcover ISBN: 978-0-9897311-0-2
Softcover ISBN: 978-0-9897311-2-6

First Edition Printed in USA.

To the many volunteers, patrons,

donors, and staff who have loved the

Michigan Theater over the years

and whose hard work and generosity

have made it what it is today

Contents

Foreword vii

CHAPTER 1   The Movies Come to Ann Arbor 1

CHAPTER 2   Ann Arbor's Own Movie Palace: The Michigan Theater 17

CHAPTER 3   From Silents to Hollywood's Golden Age 33

CHAPTER 4   Wartime and the 1940s at the Michigan Theater 49

CHAPTER 5   The 1950s 65

CHAPTER 6   The End of an Era: The 1960s and 1970s 81

CHAPTER 7   The Pipe Organ Is Reborn 97

CHAPTER 8   Citizens to the Rescue 111

CHAPTER 9   From Volunteer to Professional Organization 127

CHAPTER 10   New Leadership, New Funding, and a New Look 139

CHAPTER 11   A Restored Theater, A Revised Strategy 155

CHAPTER 12   Phase III: Restoring the Old, Creating the New 169

CHAPTER 13   An Award-Winning Community Center for the Arts 183

APPENDIX A   Gerry Hoag 203

APPENDIX B   Founding Board Members of the Michigan Community
             Theatre Corporation 213

APPENDIX C   The Barton Pipe Organ 215

             Illustration and photo credits 224

             Index 225

FOREWORD

The Michigan Theater is one of Ann Arbor's great destinations. It stands on Liberty Street just one block from the central campus of the University of Michigan. At night, the theater's blazing marquee and vertical blade sign attract a steady stream of students, townspeople, and visitors to exciting and challenging films, concerts, lectures, and special events. At the time of this publication, the theater is open 365 days a year and its two auditoriums are busy all the time.

In addition to its formidable presence, the Michigan Theater is also an outstanding historical preservation success story. Threatened in 1979 with demolition or conversion to an interior shopping mall, it was saved by the combined efforts of concerned citizens, an enlightened city government led by a dedicated mayor, a team of volunteers, and some very generous donors. In the years since, the Michigan Theater has been fully restored to its original splendor both inside and out and a contemporary screening space, new restrooms, and offices have been added to the historic structure.

Since motion pictures arrived in the 1890s, millions of words have been written about almost every aspect of their production, style, and relationship to the cultures that produced them. Very few publications, however, exist about the theaters themselves. Notable exceptions are Ben M. Hall's fascinating book, *The Best Remaining Seats: The Golden Age of the Movie Palace* (Da Capo Press, 1988), and Douglas Gomery's extensive study of American film exhibition, *Shared Pleasures: A History of Movie Presentation in the United States* (University of Wisconsin Press, 1992).

In addition to these outstanding books there have been a few photo books about individual motion picture theaters, such as Birmingham's *The Alabama Theatre: Showplace of the South* (Birmingham Landmarks, 2002) by Cecil Whitmire and Jeanne Hanks; Richmond, Virginia's *The Byrd* (Dementi Milestone Publishing, 2008) by George A. Bruner Jr.; and *The Radio City Music Hall: An Affectionate History of the World's Greatest Theater* (Dutton, 1979) by Charles Francisco. But none of these works has constituted a thorough and detailed study of one movie palace from its construction until the present.

Therefore, when Russ Collins, executive director of the Michigan Theater, suggested in 2007 that I write a book about the theater, I saw an opportunity to fill a glaring omission in film scholarship.

My interest in movie theaters began in childhood, when I frequented the beautiful Tivoli Theater in Chattanooga, Tennessee. In March 1963, while a student at the University of North Carolina, I read an early edition of Ben M. Hall's *The Best Remaining Seats* and was particularly fascinated with the chapter on theater pipe organs. Never having heard one, I was anxious to find out more about this curious instrument.

As luck would have it, just a few weeks later I attended a concert performed on the newly restored Robert Morton organ at the Center Theater in Durham, North Carolina. The organist for that evening, Don Hall, became a great friend and taught me the rudiments of theater organ performance. That summer, I visited Ben M. Hall (no relation to Don Hall) in New York and attended a show at Radio City Music Hall for the first time. Seeing this magnificent theater and hearing its "Mighty Wurlitzer" theater organ further fed my interest in the history of motion picture theaters.

Since moving to Ann Arbor, I have been involved with the Michigan Theater as an organist, board member, and volunteer. Some of the information in this book, therefore, comes from personal recollections–but these go only so far. Fortunately, there are abundant documents and photographs pertaining to the Michigan Theater that I was able to consult. Some of those, including minutes of Michigan Theater board meetings, are in archives located in the theater itself. Others are in the Gerald H. Hoag papers and W.S. Butterfield Collection at Bentley Historical Library on the North Campus of the University of Michigan. Fortunately, past issues of *The Ann Arbor News*, its predecessors, and the *Ann Arbor Observer* have been preserved on microfilm, and I had easy access to all of them. Other valuable documents were provided by organist Newton Bates and by Barbara Cook, who gave me a complete run of "Notes from the Michigan," a monthly publication of the local American Theater Organ Society group produced between 1972 and 1982.

In addition, I interviewed many people who have been or are presently associated with the Michigan Theater. These include former manager Fred Caryl; former Ann Arbor Mayor Lou Belcher; theater organ enthusiasts David and Jo Lau, Grant and Barbara Cook, Norman Hornung, and Bruce Amrine; and former Michigan Theater employees Deb Polich, Gayle Steiner, and Jill McDonough. I also interviewed several present employees, including Russ Collins, Laura Gabriel, Walt Bishop, Lee Berry, Scott Clarke, and Chris Tabacza. Judy Rumelhart and Del Dunbar also provided invaluable information. John Briggs, former president of International Alliance of Theatrical Stage Employees Union Local 395, and Karen Young, former director of the University of Michigan Office of Major Events, were especially helpful in recalling the early days of the Michigan Theater Foundation's operations in 1979 and 1980.

Another important source for this book was a "calendar" – a day-by-day list of everything that ran at the Michigan Theater from January 5, 1928, to the present. This database was prepared over several years by students in my film history class at Eastern Michigan University. To all of the students who sat for hours in front of microfilm readers to gather this information, I am extremely grateful.

This book would not have been possible without the support of Dennis Beagen, head of the Department of Communication, Media & Theatre Arts at Eastern Michigan University, and Ted Ligibel, director of EMU's Historic Preservation Program. Both provided me with necessary time and research assistance.

Many thanks also to EMU student interns Leslie VanVeen, Ann Stevenson, and David Rash, who transferred the hard copy of the "Michigan Theater Calendar" to a searchable database, and Megan Riznikove and Shannon Alden, who found additional information about the theater in *The Ann Arbor News*. U-M School of Communication interns Barbara Pezet and James Perry went through stacks of material in the theater's archives and prepared finding aids for them; their work was extremely helpful.

Finally, I want to thank Russ Collins, who made valuable additions to the text, editor Domenica Trevor, designer Marty Somberg, Alexa Selph, who prepared the index, and Bob Land for final proofreading.

THE MOVIES COME
TO ANN ARBOR

THE MICHIGAN THEATER
AND OFFICE BUILDING IN
THE LATE 1920S. BHL

O N AN APRIL EVENING in 1896, something extraordinary happened at Koster and Bial's Music Hall in New York City. The customary eighth act of a vaudeville bill was replaced by a series of short films shown by Thomas Alva Edison to demonstrate his first motion picture projector, the Vitascope. An amazed audience watched two young women performing an umbrella dance, waves breaking against a sandy beach, a burlesque boxing match, a comic allegory called "The Monroe Doctrine," a brief view of a farce called "The Milk White Flag," and, finally, a skirt dance performed by a tall blonde.

During the next four years, motion pictures would become regular features on vaudeville programs and find audiences in public auditoriums, opera houses, and amusement parks. While first available only in large cities, movies would spread across America as traveling projectionists followed the tradition of magic-lantern artists and brought films to communities across the country.

Motion pictures arrived in Ann Arbor on September 26, 1904, with the first screening of *The Great Train Robbery*,[1] an Edison production whose popularity was fueled by the recently publicized Wild West adventures of Butch Cassidy and the Sundance Kid. *The Great Train Robbery*, which would become the best-remembered short film of its era because of its innovative use of editing, was the last item on the program at the Light Infantry Armory on Ashley and West Huron streets; it followed vaudeville acts that included "The Great Gay, King of Handcuffs" and "Master

Harry Carroll, the phenomenal boy tenor."[2] The film's depiction of a passenger train holdup, the *Ann Arbor Argus-Democrat* reported the next day, "required no great stretch of the imagination for the spectator to persuade himself that he was looking at a bit from real life."[3]

NICKELODEONS

The realism remarked upon by that *Argus-Democrat* reviewer began drawing larger audiences to films around the country. Soon, movies were competing with vaudeville and found a new home in theaters built exclusively for them. Beginning in 1902 and accelerating dramatically over the next few years, entrepreneurs converted retail storefronts into small theaters devoted to the showing of films; by 1912, there were more than 10,000 of them across America. With a screen at one end, a few chairs, a piano, and a box office at the street entrance, these theaters became the principal venues for cinema. Charging five or 10 cents admission, they became known as "nickelodeons."

The most prominent feature of nickelodeons was a highly decorated facade that often included flashing electric lights. Billboards showed vivid – sometimes lurid – scenes from the films; outside some nickelodeons, a barker would invite passersby into the dark interior. A typical nickelodeon program consisted of several 10-minute, one-reel films; a song slide presentation, in which a singer performed a few popular songs and the lyrics were projected onto the theater's screen to encourage the audience to join in; and perhaps a few advertisements. A vaudeville act or two might also be performed, but the live show now took second billing to the film. While some civic leaders were bemoaning the negative influence of nickel theaters, Americans by the millions were going to the movies.

Like most communities of its size, Ann Arbor had several nickelodeons. The first was the Theatorium – billed as "Ann Arbor's Pioneer Picture Theater" – which opened in November 1906 at 119 East Liberty Street (much later, it would be the location of Liberty Street Video). According to Ann Arbor historian Grace Shackman, the Theatorium "showed three short movies for 5 cents, changing the offerings three times a week."[4]

A few weeks after the Theatorium's debut, the Casino opened at 339 South Main Street (later, the location of the Real Seafood Company). The People's Popular Family Theater, later known as the Vaudette, opened soon after at 220 South State Street. In an attempt to counter the negative

THE STAR THEATER RIOT. BHL

image of nickelodeons, the Casino advertised that "it would cater to women and children" and "give good clean shows which all can patronize."[5]

Locally and around the country, competition among nickel theaters became intense.

In late 1906 and 1907, two more venues entered the Ann Arbor market. The Bijou, a vaudeville house at 209 East Washington Street, remodeled itself in 1906 to accommodate film showings, boasted "the only fireproof Poloscope picture machine in the state," and invited patrons to "come and see the cozy theater and enjoy strictly high-class, moral entertainment."[6]

The Star Theater, which opened in 1907 at 118 East Washington Street (later the site of the Arbor Brewing Company), offered vaudeville acts as well as movies and promoted itself as a source of family entertainment. But it would gain its lasting local fame as the site of a riot on March 16, 1908, involving a crowd of about 2,000 University of Michigan students. The considerable damage included the loss of the theater's piano – students hauled it to the second floor and hoisted it out a

The considerable damage included the loss of the theater's piano – students hauled it to the second floor and hoisted it out a large window.

large window. More than a dozen students were taken to jail in handcuffs, and the fire department lost large lengths of hose to clever students who carried it off.

Accounts of the riot's cause vary (the report published in the *Ann Arbor News Argus* the next day gave a rather vague explanation). Mike Logghe, author of *True Crimes and the History of the Ann Arbor Police Department*, writes that "the riot began as a student protest against [Star Theater] manager Albert Reynolds, who allegedly had tried to win a large bet by getting a U-M football player to throw a game"[7] But another account, appearing in *The Ann Arbor News* in 1942, gives live narration of a silent film a key role:

> The trouble started when the "voice" of a silent motion picture was interrupted. The voice was Jacob Schlimmer, a burly usher, who stood in the rear of the auditorium and droned out a verbal accompaniment to the film. It was a tense moment. "Frantically," recited the voice, "the hero chews the cord that binds his wrists as he struggles to free himself and save the fair maiden from a fate that is worse than death. Will he save her?" …

> Another voice, that one from the front of the theater, sang out: "He will if he's been cleaning his teeth with Rubiform toothpaste!!"

> Schlimmer was an ex pug. He strode down the aisle, identified a university student as the author of the interruption, smashed the boy on the jaw, pounded him with lefts and rights to the face until the student slumped to the floor unconscious. A second student rose to his aid and was likewise slapped to the floor unconscious.

> The grapevine quivered and, within minutes, lines of students were coming down East Washington Street, East Liberty, and East William Street. Schlimmer? He disappeared with the first sign of trouble.

THE ORPHEUM THEATER.

BHL

Ann Arbor has never knowingly seen him since. The first voice of Ann Arbor's silent motion pictures simply walked off into silence, and was never heard again.[8]

No matter the cause of the disturbance, the Star Theater reopened for business the next day.

MOVIE PALACES

By 1911, films were becoming longer and more expensive and, as a result, each screening had to generate more revenue. Exhibitors responded by building larger theaters that could hold more people for each showing and designed these theaters to attract wealthier patrons. Film historians call these more elegant buildings "movie palaces," and they would soon supplant the ubiquitous nickelodeons as the preferred venues for motion pictures. Scholars point to the Regent Theater, which opened on the corner of Seventh Avenue and 116th Street in Manhattan in February 1913, as the first of the movie palaces. The last to go up was Radio City Music Hall, which opened on December 27, 1932, at New York's Rockefeller Center.

THE WUERTH THEATER
ORGAN. BHL

The movie palaces appealed to a desire among the middle classes for elegance. They were often designed in the style of grand European opera houses, with sweeping balconies, box seats, plush curtains, chandeliers, and other extravagant decoration. They offered every amenity, from good sight lines and air cooling to corps of well-trained ushers. The program at a movie palace would begin with a stage show; the film that followed would be accompanied by a symphony orchestra supplemented by a theater pipe organ.

While somewhat modest by movie-palace standards, the Orpheum was the first Ann Arbor theater designed exclusively for motion pictures. It opened on October 21, 1913, with a stage show featuring the Musical Dewitts and a screening of *The Hills of Strife.* The theater, built by local clothier J. Fred Wuerth at 336 South Main Street (later the site of Gratzi restaurant), seated approximately 800 people and had a balcony and box seats; its arched façade was reminiscent of Louis Sullivan's 1889 Auditorium Building in Chicago.

In October 1914, near a tailor's shop at the end of an arcade on 715 North University Avenue, the Arcade Theater opened with a program of one- and two-reel films: *Weights and Measures, Love's Refrain, A Daughter of the Plains,* and *Well! Well!* In 1917, Arcade owner Selby Moran added 17 rows of seats to the original 26, plus a balcony and box seats. Clearly, Moran was looking to add a bit of movie-palace grandeur to the modest theater. Another small, movies-only theater appeared on September 11, 1915. The Rae, a 385-seat venue at 113 West Huron Street, took its title from the initial letters of the owners' first names: Russell Dobson, Alan Stanchfield, and Emil Calman. Stanchfield managed the theater single-handedly – from taking tickets to running the projector – and eventually bought out his partners.

Wuerth built another theater – and named it after himself – next door to his Orpheum Theater on Main Street. The Wuerth and Orpheum were laid out in an L-shaped configuration with separate entrances and a common stage. The Wuerth, with more than 1,000 seats somewhat larger than the Orpheum, opened on May 12, 1917, with a feature film titled *The Valentine Girl.* According to *The Daily Times News:*

> The majority of those who view the new theater for the first time will be more than surprised at the artistic decorations, the well-planned building, and, probably most of all, at the new pipe organ which has just been installed. In addition to the program of pictures, a well-balanced musical program has been chosen, both for the organ and the augmented orchestra. The first performance will begin at 1 p.m. and last continuously until 11. There will be an organ recital by a Detroit organist before the first show.

The "pipe organ" at the Wuerth was, in actuality, a small instrument with a piano keyboard from which a piano and a few ranks of pipes could be played.[9]

THE ARCADE THEATER. BHL

THE WHITNEY THEATER. BHL

THE WHITNEY AND THE MAJESTIC

In considering the early Ann Arbor movie palaces, the Whitney Theater and the Majestic Theater deserve special mention.

The Whitney, originally called Hill's Opera House, went up in August 1871 as part of a building at 117-119 North Main Street that also contained the Earle Hotel. Constructed with a fashionable mansard roof during a national frenzy of theater building that followed the Civil War, its first presentation was a local production called *The Spy of Shiloh.* In 1908 the theater was purchased by B.C. Whitney, who added two stories and remodeled the interior in a neo-Renaissance style with imported chandeliers and Italian marble floors. The renamed Whitney Theater featured two balconies and 35 box seats and could hold more than 1,500 people. For almost 30 years, the Whitney was a legitimate theater that hosted such notables as Edwin Booth, John and Ethel Barrymore, Helen Hayes, and Alfred Lunt. It was also the home for a number of Michigan Union Opera productions including the first, *Michigenda,* in February 1908.

With the advent of motion pictures, the Whitney joined the ranks of theaters adding movies to their programming. And it scored a coup with its screening of D.W. Griffith's Civil War epic, *The Birth of a Nation*, on May 18-19, 1917. Griffith personally selected each venue on the national tour to guarantee only the most elegant settings for the film, which traveled with its own orchestra to perform the original score by Griffith and Joseph Carl Briel. Tickets were $1.50 – an extraordinary price for admission when a seat at the movies typically cost a nickel or a dime.[10]

In 1907, lumberyard owner Charles Sauer converted a roller-skating rink at 316 Maynard Street (later the site of a parking structure) into the Majestic Theater. While movies were to figure prominently in its future, the Majestic was originally built for live theater and vaudeville. It featured leather-covered mahogany seats for 1,150 patrons, four box seats on each side of the proscenium arch, and an auditorium floor that was slanted to guarantee good sight lines.[11] The program for opening night, December 19, 1907, was a performance of *The Girl of the Golden West*, a play by the great theater producer David Belasco.[12] *The Ann Arbor Daily Times* reviewer wrote the next day:

THE MAJESTIC THEATER STAFF (GERRY HOAG, THIRD FROM LEFT). BHL

The close attention given the scenes and the repeated applause at the end of each act indicated that the people who saw the play last night enjoyed the presentation. ... The music furnished deserves special mention. Five numbers were played including the "Victors," "Star Spangled Banner," and "The Time, the Place, and the Girl."

The Majestic presented vaudeville and theatrical plays (with an occasional production by University of Michigan students); films were seldom shown until the summer of 1912, when the theater began to schedule them frequently.[13] By 1917, movies were a regular offering at the Majestic and by the early 1920s supplanted vaudeville as the main attraction.

In 1919, Butterfield transferred Gerald Hoag from Saginaw, where he was a company auditor, to manage the Majestic. There, Hoag booked films and some stage acts – including performances in the 1920s by Broadway stars like Jack Benny and then-unknowns like Fred Waring. While newcomer Waring's four-day gig in 1922 was sold out, the crowd for Benny's debut performance in Ann Arbor was sparse. "Something's wrong," the comic joked upon taking the stage, "I gave out more passes than this."[14]

The Majestic was a popular theater, and its offerings were always described in display advertisements from the 1910s and 1920s as "high class," "polite," and "advanced." The Majestic was regarded as Ann Arbor's most elegant theater until the Michigan opened in 1928.

W. S. BUTTERFIELD

By the mid 1920s, film exhibition in the United States had become dominated by five large conglomerates, each with flagship theaters in major American cities. The largest of the theater chains was Paramount Publix, with approximately 500 theaters, followed by First National/Warner Bros. Loews' the exhibition branch of the Metro-Goldwyn-Mayer studios, controlled the New York market; Fox Film Corp. and, by the end of the decade, RKO had their own theaters, too.[15] The chains were vertically integrated: Each operated its own production studios, distribution network, and theaters–an efficient organization that enabled standardized products and centralized control. Paramount Publix, for example, specified the kind of pipe organ for each theater (a Mighty Wurlitzer), the ideal temperatures for the balcony, and the look of newspaper advertising. The national conglomerates also established affiliations with independent theaters and regional theater chains. One of those was W.S. Butterfield Theatres Inc., a chain that operated small and mid-size theaters in Michigan.

Walter Scott Butterfield was born in Connorsville, Indiana; when he was a boy, his family moved to Columbus, Ohio. Butterfield's father worked for the *Ohio State Journal* and Butterfield, too, began a career in journalism. Next door to the newspaper's offices, however, was the Grand Opera House, and soon young Butterfield took a job there as a program boy. Quick promotions followed – to usher, doorman, assistant treasurer – until, in 1891 at age 21, Butterfield was the treasurer of the Grand Opera House and an affiliated theater. Two years later, he took his talents to Chicago,[16] and in 1904 was promoting the construction of the Henry Boyle Theater in Fond du Lac, Wisconsin. There, he gained experience in the operation of vaudeville theaters.

Butterfield's move to Michigan came in 1907, when he purchased the Hamblin Opera House in Battle Creek and converted it to vaudeville. Before long, he owned a statewide circuit of eight theaters – just

Butterfield's move to Michigan came in 1907, when he purchased the Hamblin Opera House in Battle Creek and converted it to vaudeville. Before long, he owned a statewide circuit of eight theaters.

the right size to attract strong acts for one-week engagements. Among the performers who played the Butterfield vaudeville circuit were comedian Chic Sale (at $35 per week) and Ben Turpin, the cross-eyed comedian of early motion pictures. In 1914, Butterfield added motion pictures to his vaudeville programs and began to build movie theaters; the next step was the affiliation with Paramount Publix in 1925. By 1928, the circuit had 74 playhouses in key Michigan cities outside Detroit, including Battle Creek, East Lansing, Grand Rapids, Kalamazoo, Traverse City, Ypsilanti, and Ann Arbor.

What became of these early Ann Arbor movie theaters? "By 1912," writes Shackman, "all three nickelodeons were gone – the Theatorium became a photography studio, the Casino a grocery store, and the Vaudette a shoemaker's shop."[17] The Bijou closed in 1915 and the Star, later renamed the Columbia, closed in 1919.

By the mid-1920s, the owners of the Orpheum, Wuerth, Arcade, and Majestic had sold their operations to W.S. Butterfield Theatres Inc.; the Whitney became part of the chain in 1936. The Rae continued to operate as an independent theater until 1929, when it burned.[18] Butterfield would hold a virtual monopoly on film exhibition in the city until the 1980s, and was to play a central role in the operation of the Michigan Theater.

NOTES

[1] Grace Shackman, "Cinema's First Century: The Rise, Fall, and Revival of Ann Arbor's Downtown Theaters." *Ann Arbor Observer,* September 2003, pp. 39-45.

[2] *Ann Arbor Argus-Democrat,* September 26, 1904. Also on the program were "Eugene Henry, the minstrel boy"; "the Three Campbells in a comedy act"; "Kitty Hart, the sweet Southern singer"; and the novelty club jugglers Whitlark and Young.

[3] Ibid. "The train robbery pictures represented the hold-up of a passenger train in the West. The whole thing was shown with wonderful realism, how the robbers stopped the train, relieved the passengers of their valuables, made their escape, were pursued, fired upon and killed. The scene was decidedly realistic, and it required no great stretch of the imagination for the spectator to persuade himself that he was looking at a bit from real life."

[4] Shackman, *Ann Arbor Observer,* September 2003.

[5] Ibid.

[6] *The Ann Arbor Weekly Argus* of December 31, 1906, reported: "The Bijou will close the year by re-opening. Much new paint, new seats, and new scenery, will make the place a very pleasant one to spend the evening. The only fireproof Poloscope picture machine in the state will make its home in the theater. Mr. I.E. Rosenthal of the Chicago Conservatory of Music will have charge of the illustrated songs. Prof. William Schwartz, a professional pianist, will act as musical director."

[7] Mike Logghe, *True Crimes and the History of the Ann Arbor Police Department (2002):* "When protesters failed to get Reynolds to come out (reports differ on whether he exited through the back door or was hiding in the basement), they began throwing bricks stolen from a construction site across the street. The riot lasted all night, in spite of appeals by both law dean Henry Hutchins and U-M president James Angell. Eighteen students were arrested, but charges were later dropped when they agreed to raise money for repairs."

[8] *The Ann Arbor News,* March 17, 1942.

[9] In the late 1920s the console was tricked out by adding a few decorations intended to make the instrument look like the Barton pipe organ in the new Michigan Theater.

[10] *The Birth of a Nation* has been critically acclaimed for its technical excellence, its considerable length for its time, and for the sweep and grandeur with which it depicted the Civil War. But its portrayals of African Americans drew vigorous protests from the NAACP and other civil rights groups. The controversy simply

fueled the film's popularity, but the stark racism in *The Birth of a Nation* continues to cast a shadow over this seminal motion picture.

[11] *The Ann Arbor Daily Times* of December 19, 1907, reported: "Never was there a greater transformation than has been effected in the large brick building on Maynard Street which has been converted from a fine skating rink into one of the coziest and prettiest little theaters in the state. . . . Everything is new, comfortable, and up-to-date."

[12] Following the opening production, the Majestic scheduled vaudeville acts through the powerful theatrical producers and agents Klaw and Earlanger. When W.S. Butterfield Theatres Inc. took over management of the house in early 1908, vaudeville acts were booked through the vaudeville producer and agent B.F. Keith.

[13] *The Daily Times News* of July 21, 1912, reported: "Starting again tonight the Majestic Theater will return to its regular summer policy of Kinemacolor motion pictures and photoplays de luxe. . . . Several big special features have been secured for this week, and as usual Kinemacolor New York and Parisian fashions will be exhibited for the benefit of the ladies tonight. Tomorrow night one of the greatest of all motion pictures will be shown in a pictorial representation of 'Lincoln's Gettysburg Address.' This picture is beautiful beyond description, and as an object lesson in history and patriotism has never been surpassed. It is colored and presented in a high-class manner."

[14] *The Ann Arbor News*, October 6, 1944.

[15] Paramount Publix was created in 1925 by a merger of Paramount Pictures and the Chicago theater chain of Balaban and Katz. First National was formed when a group of independent theaters merged to better compete with Paramount Publix, and, later in the decade, acquired the Warner Brothers Pictures theater chain. RKO was established by RCA on the remains of the defunct Keith-Orpheum vaudeville circuit.

[16] Butterfield moved to Chicago to work at the Academy of Music, later became a road manager for the Charles E. Blaney Co., and was part owner and manager for Rose Stahl, who would go on to vaudeville stardom.

[17] Shackman, *Ann Arbor Observer*, September 2003.

[18] The Arcade, which was operating as a second-run theater by the late 1920s, suffered the same fate a year earlier: On the morning of December 26, 1928, with its posters advertising Charles Chaplin's *The Circus* as the next attraction, it was gutted by fire.

THE WUERTH THEATER. BHL

CHAPTER 2

ANN ARBOR'S OWN MOVIE PALACE: THE MICHIGAN THEATER

B Y THE MIDDLE OF the Roaring Twenties, almost 100 million people a week were going to the movies – and the nation's theater chains responded with a wave of movie-palace construction around the country. The trend that had begun 15 years before reached its pinnacle with the opening of mammoth theaters such as the New York Roxy and the Fox Theaters in Brooklyn, Atlanta, Detroit, St. Louis, and San Francisco. Often seating more than 5,000 people and featuring extravagant architecture, lavish service, full stage facilities, large orchestra pits, and fabulous pipe organs, these "cathedrals of the motion picture" offered a new and grand kind of entertainment.

At the larger theaters, the "presentation," as it was often called, would begin with an overture by the orchestra, followed by an organ solo, several acts of vaudeville, and usually a lavish and visually stunning finale with an on-stage ensemble of singers, dancers, and vaudeville stars. The feature film came next, accompanied by the theater's symphony orchestra, the pipe organ, or both. Movie palaces in smaller towns might present a few acts of vaudeville, a solo by a small pit orchestra or piano, and perhaps a few song slides accompanied by the pianist before the film – less grand than big-city presentations, but just as popular.

One of the outstanding features of the Michigan Theater was that it did not look like other movie palaces of its era.

The time was ripe for Ann Arbor to have a true movie palace of is own. The city was growing and civic leaders recognized that the rapidly growing University of Michigan, rather than manufacturing, was the community's chief asset. In 1922, a master plan for the city's development prepared by the Olmsted Brothers of New York suggested street improvements and a zoning policy that would allow for growth while preserving the open, spacious character of the city. While ignoring many of the recommendations of the Olmsted plan, the city council did pass a zoning ordinance in August 1923 that gave direction to downtown construction.[1]

Enrollment at U-M in the 1920s had reached 10,000, but the campus was able to comfortably accommodate only half that number. The Michigan Legislature responded by doubling the university's annual appropriation and approving millions of dollars for land purchase and construction. Angell Hall, the William L. Clements Library, Michigan Stadium, the first portion of the Law Quad, and additions to the University Hospital were built during this period; the Michigan League was under construction and plans were in place for new dormitories. In 1927, the Board of Regents prohibited students from operating automobiles except in "exceptional and extraordinary cases." As a result, the central campus area had a growing and captive audience.[2]

AN OPPORTUNITY SEIZED

Noting the emerging business opportunities in the campus area, local entrepreneur Angelo Poulos decided to demolish four houses he owned on Liberty Street and use the space to construct an office building. Work began in the summer of 1926, but a few months into the project Poulos added a movie palace to his plans. Rather than operate the theater as a family enterprise, Poulos contracted with W.S. Butterfield Theatres Inc., which was already operating the Majestic, Wuerth, Orpheum, and Arcade theaters in town. Butterfield would help Poulos plan the new theater and operate it as its flagship house in Ann Arbor.[3]

On June 15, 1927, construction of the Michigan Theater began on the north side of Liberty Street on a plot just behind the Pouloses' office building, with an entrance corridor running to Liberty Street. An addition to the office building would be built over the theater entrance and to the east so that eventually the entrance would run through the office building to Liberty Street.

To design the theater Poulos hired Maurice Finkel, who as an architect for the Albert Kahn organization had designed several theaters as well as office and apartment buildings in the Detroit area. Finkel recently had gone into business for himself and had designed a number of other theaters and commercial buildings;[4] his design for Ann Arbor's new movie palace would be an independent effort. The choice of a local architect instead of a national firm specializing in movie theaters[5] would ultimately ensure that the Michigan Theater's appearance would be truly distinctive.

Finkel's design won praise from *The Ann Arbor Daily News*:

> Cognizant of the fact that Ann Arbor is one of the great educational and intellectual centers, Mr. Finkel felt it incumbent upon him to design not merely another fine theater, but rather to create a shrine to art, one that would be in harmony with the cultural atmosphere of the University. … [T]he very character of Ann Arbor, as a university town, with its classical and especially medieval styles in architecture, with its academic buildings and fraternity houses, suggests a certain historical motif demanding the selection of the Romanesque style of architecture with its opportunity for beautiful surface ornamentation and its deep reveals in its column settings. This character of architecture is skillfully and masterfully carried out through the entire exterior and interior of the building.[6]

Indeed, one of the outstanding features of the Michigan Theater was that it did not look like other movie palaces of its era. Its interior was rather spartan compared to the excesses of many other theaters, and the generous use of dark wainscoting in both the lobby and auditorium was also unusual. The layout of the auditorium was longer and more narrow than that of most movie palaces, which tended, like theaters designed for live performances, to be wide and shallow so that all seats were as close to the stage as possible.

THE ORIGINAL MARQUEE
AND VERTICAL BLADE. BHL

Still, the Michigan Theater exhibited many features common to other movie palaces. The ornate façade, facing Liberty Street, held a rectangular marquee and a vertical sign that spelled out the theater's name. (The vertical sign was, oddly, somewhat oversized; perhaps it was originally intended for another Michigan Theater or, instead of a custom job, was ordered from a manufacturer who produced only a few standard sizes.) In any case, the façade of the Michigan Theater would "be a blaze of lights," *The Ann Arbor Daily News* reported. "So large is the giant electrically illuminated sign . . . and so much current does it consume, that a special ordinance had to be passed by city council to permit the management to erect and operate it."[7]

Beneath the marquee were wood-framed doors with glass fronts and brass fixtures. The box office was on the right side of the outer lobby, from which a gradually sloping floor ended at a second set of doors. Those opened onto the grand foyer and a double staircase that led to the balcony. The foyer was illuminated by chandeliers and sconces, and beveled mirrors on the upper level gave the illusion of a much larger space. That second level featured two entry corridors to the balcony and two sets of stairs that could be used for exiting the theater; restrooms, offices, and storage areas were also on the foyer's second level.

The auditorium joined the foyer at a 90-degree angle, and patrons entered it through four sets of doors. The main floor sloped gently downward toward the orchestra pit; restrained medallions and small chandeliers decorated the ceiling and dark wainscoting covered the side walls under the balcony. Moving out from under that balcony, a patron looking up would have seen five golden arches on either side of the proscenium that marked the grills through which the pipe organ spoke. Beneath these grills were arched exits on either side, although the one closest to the stage was the only functional one. Niches intended to hold illuminated art objects were tucked between the two exit arches.

THE MICHIGAN THEATER
ORCHESTRA, KARL
WEIDERHOLD,
CONDUCTOR. BHL

The stage was 61 feet wide and 28 feet deep with a proscenium opening 25 feet 7 inches high and 34 feet 9 inches wide. A resistance dimmer board controlled the lighting. There were 35 lines to hang curtains, set pieces, and the movie screen. An asbestos fire curtain emblazoned with a large blue "M" could be lowered in front of the red house curtain. There were three dressing rooms on the stage level and three more on a second floor. The dressing room for the chorus was in the basement, along with a common area, storage, and, deep below the stage, boilers and a well that provided water to cool the theater's air supply.

Below the foot of the stage was the orchestra pit, which could hold about 15 musicians. Lacking an elevator, it was accessed from the basement through a greenroom for the musicians with a small door that opened into the orchestra pit. On the left side of the pit was the Barton pipe organ, mounted on its own lift that could raise it to stage level for solo performances.

When it opened on January 5, 1928, the Michigan was easily the most splendid of Ann Arbor's movie theaters and the only one equipped to offer the elaborate stage presentations by then common at American movie palaces.

Unseen by patrons but vital to the quality of the film presentation was the theater's modern projection booth. It was equipped with two high-intensity, 35-millimeter carbon-arc projectors; a Brenograph machine for projecting slides and special effects; and a theatrical follow spot for stage acts. The booth had extra-thick walls and metal doors that could cover projection ports in case of fire – a particular threat to theaters in an era when films were printed on highly explosive nitrate-based stock – as well as an escape ladder so the projectionist could make a hasty exit across the theater's roof.

The Ann Arbor Daily News marveled at one of the new projectors' notable features:

> The old custom of switching from one machine to another by hand has been discontinued and one touch of a foot lever, electrically controlled, makes the change – which is so fast that it is impossible to detect it in the audience.[8]

OPENING NIGHT

When it opened on January 5, 1928, the Michigan was easily the most splendid of Ann Arbor's movie theaters and the only one equipped to offer the elaborate stage presentations by then common at American movie palaces.[9] The presentation, reported *The Ann Arbor Daily News* on January 5, 1928,

is really a newer form of what was once known as "variety" shows, and now constitutes a higher class form of amusement than vaudeville. ... Aside from the picture and stage attraction, there will be the usual line of screen short subjects, and special orchestral and organ selections, all combining to make up a balanced bill that should prove popular with Ann Arbor audiences.[10]

As the opening night approached, congratulatory advertisements from local merchants appeared in *The Daily News.* The arrival of this new theater was enthusiastically embraced as a boon to the campus retail area and the community as a whole. On the eve of the opening, a *Daily News* editorial touched on the new theater's potential: "It is a masterpiece of playhouse construction and art" with "accommodations and conveniences that would enable any large legitimate production to play before an Ann Arbor audience."[11]

In anticipation of big opening-night attendance, Butterfield sold Michigan Theater tickets at the Majestic and Wuerth and scheduled two complete performances, at 7 and 9 p.m.

Crowds assembled early for the first show; lines stretched two blocks down Liberty Street.[12] As they entered the theater, patrons saw many familiar faces. Standing at the front door was the popular manager of

the Majestic Theater, Gerald Hoag, whom Butterfield had brought over to the new theater along with other key Majestic staff, including box office manager Lois Grandberg and orchestra leader Karl Weiderhold. W.S. Butterfield himself was present along with his company's general manager, E.C. Beatty, and organ builder Dan Barton.

There were probably opening remarks from Butterfield, Hoag, and assembled civic leaders, although there are no newspaper accounts of them. The 11-piece Michigan Theater orchestra played an overture especially written for the occasion. Assisting the orchestra at the pipe organ was Floyd Hoffman, an employee of the Barton Organ Co. sent from Chicago; it was customary for the manufacturer to provide an organist for the first days of a theater's opening. Even with Barton on hand to make sure that all went well with his latest installation, there was a snag. The organ console became stuck in the "up" position on the lift, Barton recalled many years later, and during the opening remarks Hoffman whispered to him loudly: "How do I get this damned thing down?"

The opening-night program featured Ida Mae Chadwick and Her Dizzy Blondes in a stage production called *From Rags to Riches*, followed by the feature film, *A Hero for a Night*. The 60-minute romantic comedy from Universal Studios starred popular silent-film actors Glenn Tryon and Patsy Ruth Miller.[13] Also in the cast was a pet monkey, which created an opportunity for some typical promotional foolishness. "No opening is without its humorous episodes," *The Daily News* reported,

> … and last night's was no exception. A monkey caused more commotion, fun and fright than one small animal on pleasure bent has any right to do. Somehow or other, he got in for the first performance (maybe he heard that Billy, one of his hairy friends, was starring in the picture and wanted to take a good look) but at any rate, he was there and proceeded to seat himself in the nice soft curves of a lady's arm to watch the show, much to her consternation.

OPPOSITE: GRAND FOYER
DETAIL. MT

No less a personage than W.S. Butterfield came down to remove the offending guest, but had little success. Ushers were called to the rescue and they attempted to grab the monkey's head with a handkerchief in an effort to capture him. The animal must have thought, "Well, well, here, at last, is someone to play with me," and seized upon the handkerchief mischievously.

By this time, there was considerable laughter and excitement among the spectators seated near where the episode took place. Finally, the monkey was curled up in an usher's arm and was removed, and peace was restored.[14]

The Michigan Daily published a wry commentary on the opening the next day:

The Turkish bath school of theater architecture has a new and overwhelming triumph in the new Butterfield gift to the world of popular amusement – the Michigan. Rising nobly to the skies, behind a façade of shops and shop windows, this palace of the movie is the epitome of all efforts of its kind. It is unique in Ann Arbor, for the sole reason that it is more nearly like a theater than any other of the converted skating rinks [referring to the Majestic] which have served the intellectual audiences of the city for so long.

The bill offered deserves little comment for apparently all of the city turned out to see it. The problem now is to keep everyone you meet from telling you about it for the hundredth time.[15]

A more prophetic observation, however, came from Hoag, who wrote in the opening night's program:

The Michigan was not built for today only, but constructed in the hopes that it might be a monument for years to come and a credit to the community even when the city is many times its present size. To that end, the attractions which the theatre will present promise to be in keeping with the magnificence of the playhouse.

The Michigan Theater opened as Ann Arbor's most impressive venue for films and was to remain the city's only true movie palace, representing the pinnacle of motion picture theater construction in Ann Arbor.

THE MICHIGAN THEATER'S ARCHITECT, Maurice Finkel, was born in Romania in 1888 and came to the United States as a child. He received a degree in architecture in 1913 from New York's Cooper Union School for the Advancement of Science and Art; he moved to Michigan in 1915 and started his own architectural firm in Detroit. Over the next 30 years the firm designed more than 200 structures, including apartment buildings, private homes, commercial buildings, and three movie theaters in addition to the Michigan in Ann Arbor.

Two of those theaters, both in Detroit, have been demolished. The Littman-Peoples Theater was at 8208-12 12th Street; it was renamed the Abington Theater in 1945 and then the Goldcoast Theater in 1956 before closing in 1958. The Tuxedo Theater, originally called the New Yiddish Theater, was located at 11738 Hamilton Avenue. Finkel also designed Jackson's Michigan Theatre, which opened at 124 North Mechanic Street on July 1, 1930. The Jackson theater, which has been restored, shows feature films and hosts live concerts.

Finkel died in 1949 and was buried at the Machpelah Cemetery in Ferndale. The gravestone gives the date of March 15, 1950, which reflects the Jewish tradition of waiting one year after a death to place the headstone of the deceased.

MAURICE FINKEL

MAURICE FINKEL. MT

Finkel also designed Jackson's Michigan Theatre, which opened at 124 North Mechanic Street on July 1, 1930.

ANGELO POULOS AND
FAMILY. MT

ANGELO POULOS was born in Kakouri, Tripolis, Greece on May 20, 1890. Like many of his neighbors and relatives, he imigrated to the United States, arriving in New York on the steamship *Patros* on March 17, 1912.

Poulos settled in Ann Arbor, where he joined a thriving Greek community that was in the process of establishing itself in grocery, restaurant, and real estate businesses in the community. Between 1916 and 1929, Poulos operated a restaurant on South Main Street. He married his first wife Thalia in July 1923 and became a United States citizen in October 1924.

In 1926, Poulos built an office building on property he owned on the north side of East Liberty Street near its intersection with State Street. Since boyhood when he had worked as a projectionist at a small theater in his hometown, Poulos had dreamed of building an elegant movie palace. In June 1927, he began construction of the Michigan Theater on an L-shaped piece of property adjacent to the existing office building. To finance the project, Poulos took out a mortgage of $525,000. A few weeks later, he took out a second mortgage of $40,250 to pay the Otto Misch Co. and Maurice Finkel for architectural work on the proposed theater. (Misch received $35,250 and Finkel $5,000).

In 1927, Poulos entered into a business partnership with Theodore Dames, and they purchased the Ann Arbor Savings Bank in that year. In 1928, they acquired the Allenel Hotel located on the southwest corner of Ann and Huron streets. For many years, the Allenel was known as the finest hotel in the community and hosted visiting concert artists as well as the Philadelphia Orchestra.

In 1933, Poulos' wife Thalia died, and in 1934 he went to Greece where he married his second wife, Niki Michael. In 1935, Poulos donated $1,000 to help found St. Nicholas Greek Orthodox Church of which he became a prominent member.

Poulos suffered a heart attack on November 6, 1943, and died a few days later. He was survived by his wife Niki; a son, William (Bill), who was in the armed forces at the time; three daughters, Bertha, Tula, and Bessie; and three sisters. Poulos was buried at the Forest Hills Cemetery in Ann Arbor.

Shortly after Poulos began construction on the Michigan Theater in 1927, he entered into an agreement with the W.S. Butterfield Corp. to oversee the structure's fitting out as a theater and to eventually operate it. Butterfield took out a lease on the Michigan Theater that eventually was extended to a 50-year term. When that lease expired in January 1978, Butterfield notified the Poulos family that it did not intend to renew the lease. At this point, the descendants of Angelo Poulos became actively involved with developing plans to find new uses for the structure. This action led eventually to the sale of the Michigan Theater building to the Michigan Community Theater Corp.

NOTES

[1] Jonathan Marwil, *A History of Ann Arbor* (University of Michigan Press, 1991), p. 107.

[2] Ibid., p. 100.

[3] Butterfield's original 30-year lease was later extended to 50 years.

[4] Finkel, whom Poulos paid $5,000, went on to plan the Michigan Theater in Jackson in 1930.

[5] One such firm, Rapp and Rapp of Chicago, designed the Chicago Theater, Detroit's Michigan Theater, the Paramount Theater in New York's Times Square, and the Tivoli in Chattanooga, Tennessee.

[6] *The Ann Arbor Daily News*, January 5, 1928.

[7] Ibid.: Manager Gerald H. Hoag estimated "that the cost for operating the electrical appliances and fixtures alone about the theater will be more than $20 an hour."

[8] "Everything about the room from which the pictures will be projected upon the Michigan screen, is complete and the newest in modern equipment of this type," *The Ann Arbor Daily News* reported. "[I]ncluded in the projection equipment are new arc lamps of the high intensity type. These lamps each consume 15, 000 watts of current and give a brilliance of approximately 6,000,000 candlepower per lamp. So intense is the current that the carbons have to be revolved continuously by a special motor driven unit."

[9] About the "presentation" format, Hoag wrote in the program: "The Michigan will combine a vaudeville and picture policy, showing the biggest attractions on the Keith-Albee circuit in conjunction with the finest achievements in photoplays. Very few theaters in the state are better equipped to successfully stage as large productions as is this theater."

[10] *The Ann Arbor Daily News*, January 5, 1928: "The policy of the Michigan Theater as outlined by Gerald H. Hoag, manager, sponsors a stage presentation, similar to the type of stage entertainment, offered at the Michigan Theater in Detroit and other metropolitan theaters. The stage presentation is really a newer form of what was once known as 'variety' shows, and now constitutes a higher-class form of amusement than vaudeville. Paramount, Metro-Goldwyn-Mayer, First National, and Universal pictures will be shown, in accordance with the Butterfield policy that has been in practice for some time at the Majestic and Arcade theaters. Aside from the picture and stage attraction, there will be the usual line of screen short subjects, and special orchestral and organ selections, all combining to make up a balanced bill that should prove popular with Ann Arbor audiences."

[11] *The Ann Arbor Daily News*, January 4, 1928: "A new theater opens its doors tonight. It is a masterpiece of playhouse construction and art. It would be a credit to a much larger city than Ann Arbor. The new Michigan is to present stage entertainment and movies. It has stage accommodations and conveniences that would enable any large legitimate production to play before an Ann Arbor audience. The new Michigan represents 'the last word' in theaters. It has beauty, it has comfort and it has refinements which will appeal to the better tastes among the theater-going public. Nothing has been left undone, it would seem, to give the city something that will rank with the best of its kind."

[12] "Long before 7 o'clock, the time set for the first performance," *The Ann Arbor Daily News* reported, "the crowd assembled and by the time the doors were thrown open, there was a long line more than sufficient to fill every seat in the house waiting to be admitted."

[13] *A Hero for a Night* opened at New York's Colony Theater on December 25, 1927, but Butterfield publicists falsely claimed that the New York premiere had been delayed until after the film's screening at the Michigan Theater. The story, capitalizing on the recent notoriety of Charles Lindbergh, was about a young taxi driver who is taking flying lessons through a correspondence school. In his pursuit of financing, he meets a tycoon's daughter and engages in romance with the same plucky enthusiasm that he displays toward flying lessons.

[14] *The Ann Arbor Daily News*, January 6, 1928.

[15] *The Michigan Daily* editorialist continued: "The one unfortunate result of the new theater, if you call the rest fortunate, is that there will be no more vaudeville at the Majestic. It seems too bad that Ann Arbor should linger in the minds of the gods behind the Butterfield management as being too poor to sustain two 'variety' acts at the same time. Now that there is something better, I must confess to a romantic attachment for the Maj. where I've so often had my ribs nearly bashed in, and to see it sink to the level of the Arcade – a level low indeed – is a bit saddening to one who, in spite of an intellectual conviction that the movies are stupid and not worth while, finds himself regularly at the show four nights a week."

WALL DETAIL, MICHIGAN THEATER AUDITORIUM. MT

From Silents to Hollywood's Golden Age

WHEN THE MICHIGAN Theater opened its doors on January 5, 1928, the nation's film industry was enjoying unprecedented prosperity. The five major studios were producing several hundred feature films a year, and they were guaranteed a screening in the studios' owned and affiliated theaters. Silent films had reached a peak of expressiveness: Charlie Chaplin, Buster Keaton, and other gifted artists of the silent era were enormously popular. Movie theaters grand and small dotted the main streets of almost every American city, presenting motion pictures, vaudeville acts, big bands, orchestras, and organists in an atmosphere that suggested the regal surroundings of European opera houses.

The Michigan Theater's opening-night program – Ida Mae Chadwick and Her Dizzy Blondes followed by *A Hero for a Night* – represented the blend of live and film entertainment that characterized movie-palace presentations in the era. The theater settled into a presentation pattern that remained stable for the next 18 months. Varying slightly depending on the length of the film and stage show, daily matinees were at 2 (film) and 3:30 p.m. (stage show); Sunday usually meant three matinees, at 1:30 (film), 3 (stage show), and 4 p.m. (film). Evening shows were at 7 (stage show) and 8:45 p.m. (film). Weekday prices were 10, 30, and 40 cents for matinees and 10 and 50 cents for evenings. Prices were slightly higher on Sundays: Children were admitted for 25 cents and adults for 50 cents.[1]

HENRY SANTRY AND HIS
ORCHESTRA. BHL

For the price of admission, Michigan Theater audiences enjoyed a show that included musical performances, live acts, and film. A typical presentation would begin with an overture from the theater's 11-piece resident orchestra, often followed by a novelty film such as a travelogue or short comedy. The live stage show would be next, usually a vaudeville act that might blend comedy, music, and dance. Several short presentations separated the stage show from the feature film – a Kinogram (the newsreel of the silent era), an organ solo, and a performance by a small jazz band or other music ensemble. The feature film would be next, accompanied by the organ and the orchestra; an exit march performed by the theater orchestra would close the program.[2]

A list of some of the vaudeville acts that also played the Michigan Theater's stage in its earliest years opens a window onto a lost culture: Lottie Mayer and her "Disappearing Water Ballet," Harry Rogers' All-Girl Revue, Zez Confrey and his band, Charles Bennington and his New York Newsboys Harmonica Band, Buster Shaven and his Tiny Town Re-

vue ("A Merry Cyclone of Midget Frolics"), The
Hilton Sisters (conjoined twins Daisy and Vio-
let), Trixie Freganza and her "New Bag O' Trix."
A few of the acts that performed at the Michigan
in its early days went on to wider renown, including Eubie Blake and Company and Paul
Tremaine ("King of Saxophonists") and his Aris-
tocrats of Modern Music. Harry Carroll, best
known for co-writing the song *The Trail of the
Lonesome Pine*, appeared with "his new revue
– Glorifying American Youth." Another of the
few acts that 21st-century readers might recognize was The World Famous Foy Family in
"A Variety of Foyisms."[3]

The Michigan Theater's films came mostly
from Paramount and MGM. The Butterfield
chain's affiliation with Paramount Publix
meant a guaranteed supply of Paramount
films; MGM films were available to complete the theater's screening schedule. The
Michigan, like most theaters, changed its
program twice a week: The first feature was booked
Sunday through Wednesday and the second ran Thursday through
Saturday. To meet such a demanding schedule, the Michigan also screened
films from Universal, Fox, and First National/Warner Brothers. To fill the
bills at its Majestic, Orpheum, Wuerth, and Arcade theaters as well, Butterfield required access to virtually all film product available.

Today's film enthusiasts expecting to see evidence of the finest silent
dramas and comedies might be mystified by some of the titles screened
at the Michigan during its first year, including *A Girl in Every Port* (with
Louise Brooks), *Silk Legs, Home Made, A Reno Divorce, The Flaming
Youths, Finders Keepers, That's My Daddy, If I Were Single, Why Sailors
Go Wrong, The Private Life of Helen of Troy*, and *Slightly Used*. The lurid
tone of the titles might be the result of the industry's practice of censoring
content; producers must have reasoned that if the content had to be tame,
at least the titles could be suggestive. But these films represent not the special and unique, but the typical – just a sample of thousands of films that are
now, like so much of the culture of vaudeville, lost and forgotten.

Equipment Furnished and Installed by The National Theatre Supply Co. for Projection Room, Michigan Theatre, Ann Arbor, Mich.

ORIGINAL PROJECTORS. MT

Most of the films scheduled at the Michigan were "programmers" – light, enjoyable, inexpensively made films that usually ran less than 90 minutes and featured second-tier performers. The notion of motion pictures as art worthy of preservation is a relatively recent concept; thus almost none of these films survive because they were not considered valuable at the time. Distributors regularly disposed of films so that there would always be a demand for fresh product, and until the early 1950s, movies were printed on a nitrate-based film stock that was highly flammable and tended to oxidize. If they initially survived at all, prints of films literally rusted away.

EXPERIMENTS WITH SYNCHRONIZED SOUND

Since the beginning of motion pictures in the late 19th century, filmmakers and exhibitors had sought to combine synchronized sound with moving images, but the technologies were not yet available to reliably achieve precise synchronization, adequate amplification, and acceptable sound fidelity. Following the end of World War I, however, dramatic strides were made in the fields of audio recording. Developments in radio introduced microphones, amplifiers, and electrical reproduction equipment to the process of

By May 1928 Hollywood's major studios had agreed to use the Movietone sound-on-film system and the wholesale shift to sound began in earnest.

making phonograph records. Western Electric, the manufacturing division of AT&T, made particularly important progress in these areas.

By the mid-1920s the film industry was experimenting with dozens of methods of achieving synchronized motion picture sound; two emerged as most promising. The first, developed by Western Electric and sublicensed to Warner Brothers under the name Vitaphone, used 16-inch phonograph discs to hold the film's sound. Special turntables were synchronized to the speed of the film's projectors and rotated the discs at 33 1/3 revolutions per minute. While Vitaphone produced good-quality sound, its dual systems made it very easy for the sound and picture to get out of sync.

In 1925 Warner Brothers began testing the Vitaphone system at the Manhattan Opera House in New York. Warner's initial motivation was to provide a high-quality synchronized musical score for its features and filmed versions of vaudeville acts so that all of its theaters, especially the smaller ones, could offer a program of entertainment that rivaled the largest "presentation" movie palaces. In August 1926 it released *Don Juan,* a costume drama starring John Barrymore that had a synchronized score and a few sound effects. The film was a sensation. In October 1927 Warner released *The Jazz Singer*, starring Al Jolson. *The Jazz Singer* had a recorded musical accompaniment and depended upon traditional silent film subtitles except for a few sequences in which Jolson sang. In two of those sequences Jolson improvised passages of monologue, and audiences were amazed to hear natural speech coming from the screen. The response prompted Warner to move ahead with producing entirely dialogued films.

At the same time, Fox Film Corp. was developing newsreels with a method it called Movietone, which recorded the sound information directly onto the film in the form of a thin strip of exposed emulsion that registered the sound as variations in light intensity. While this sound-on-film method guaranteed perfect synchronization, its sound quality did not match Vitaphone's. The first Fox Movietone newsreel, which recorded Charles Lindbergh's landing in Paris, was screened in New York on May 21, 1927.[4] Over the next few months Fox began releasing silent features with recorded musical scores, and in September premiered F.W. Murnau's *Sunrise*, which had a recorded score plus sound effects and crowd noises.

By May 1928 Hollywood's major studios had agreed to use the Movietone sound-on-film system and the wholesale shift to sound began in earnest – five months after the opening of the Michigan Theater as a silent film/live show presentation house.[5]

ANN ARBOR'S FIRST 'TALKIES'

The Wuerth presented the first sound film in Ann Arbor – the Fox feature *The Ghost Talks*, starring Charles Eaton and Helen Twelvetrees – in March 1929. (The program also featured three Fox short films of popular vaudeville acts and a Movietone newsreel.) Dennis M. Allen, who chronicled the arrival of sound films at Ann Arbor theaters in the *Ann Arbor Observer*, speculates that they came a year or two after their introduction in other parts of the country because Butterfield held a virtual monopoly on local film exhibition and saw no need to invest in an expensive new technology until absolutely necessary.[6] George Westenfeld, a Butterfield projectionist at the time, also recalled that

> sound equipment intended for the Wuerth actually arrived in Ann Arbor early in 1928. Before it could be installed, however, it was pulled off the railroad platform and reshipped to Bay City, where another Butterfield theater urgently needed it to match a sound-equipped competitor. With production of sound equipment lagging far behind demand nationally, it was almost a year before replacements arrived.[7]

"Talkies" did well at the Wuerth, and within a few months Butterfield had wired its other theaters for synchronized sound films. The Michigan's manager, Gerry Hoag, said that his theater would soon have "talking where talking is best and silent where it is most appreciated."[8] In the first half of 1929, the Michigan Theater's projection booth was wired for both

Vitaphone and Movietone systems and sound amplifiers and speakers were installed.

The Michigan screened its last regularly scheduled silent film, along with a full vaudeville show, on June 15, 1929.[9] The next day, the theater entered a new era in its history with the screening of *Weary River*, a part-talking Vitaphone film from First National with silent star Richard Barthelmess – best remembered for his role in D.W. Griffith's 1922 *Way Down East* – in his first sound film (or not – it leaked out after the film's release that the star's singing voice was dubbed by another performer). Also on the program was the filmed short subject *In a Chinese Temple Garden*, with music by English composer Albert W. Ketelby and featuring hand-colored scenes, as well as a newsreel and organist Bob Howland's "Original Novelty Presentation" titled *The Honey Bee's Knees*.

BOB HOWLAND. MT

It appears that, like many early talking films, *Weary River* had little to commend to it other than its recorded sound (a *New York Times* critic labeled it a "banal jailbird tale" although, ironically, he praised the star's singing voice).[10] Nevertheless, the change in the Michigan's programming policy was played up in an *Ann Arbor Daily News* advertisement announcing that "Via the Michigan Talking Screen – Hundreds of Broadway Stars who would never be heard in Ann Arbor will come to you!"

With the screening of *Weary River*, the programmatic blend of live entertainment and movies would see a decade-long decline at the Michigan Theater – one that largely mirrored a nationwide trend. Through the 1930s, live performance diminished as a presence on the stages and orchestra pits of movie palaces across the country as two forces – the Great Depression and the arrival of talking motion pictures – reshaped the American entertainment industry. In hundreds of theaters, musicians lost their jobs as orchestras were steadily disbanded and pipe organ consoles were lowered from view for the last time. Job opportunities for film accompanists dried up and, one by one, manufacturers of theater organs shut down their factories. Only a few large theaters in major metropolitan areas kept their stage shows going, eventually leaving only Radio City Music Hall to present the once-common movie/live show program.[11]

It was expensive to recruit performers and maintain an orchestra, pipe organ, and stage crew. Before the shift to recorded sound, the Michigan Theater's account books show that payroll averaged $900 per week. Without a stage crew and the resident orchestra, those expenses dropped by almost half, to $500 a week. The cost of vaudeville acts and film rental averaged $1,500 a week; without vaudeville, that tab dropped to $900. A week without live shows saved the Michigan an average of $1,000.

Still, the combined live show and film was a familiar model that exhibitors were slow to abandon entirely. The Michigan Theater showed only talking films for the remainder of the summer of 1929[12] – Walt Disney's landmark *Steamboat Willie*, the animated film with synchronized music and sound effects that introduced Mickey Mouse, played the Michigan on July 18 – but in the fall live entertainment returned to the Michigan as students returned to the University of Michigan campus. For the rest of the year, the theater was again featuring regularly scheduled live entertainment, including the Michigan Union Opera's *Music-Go-Round*, the first time the group's annual performance was presented on the Michigan stage.[13]

BIG NAMES ON MICHIGAN'S STAGE

The Michigan's Thanksgiving week musical revue brought Jack Benny back to town as master of ceremonies for *Tanned Legs*. Manager Hoag, who had booked Benny's disappointing appearance at the Majestic Theater in the 1920s, remembered the Michigan Theater visit well: He gave Benny $500 to continue onto his next engagement in Chicago after the performer lost all his money betting on horses. Indeed, the Michigan's surviving account books record – in Hoag's meticulous longhand – that Benny received precisely $535.70 for his November appearance and that the William Morris Agency was paid $142.85 for booking him. It was in Chicago that Benny attracted the attention of promoters who later gave him the opportunity to sign a radio contract. Over the next 20 years Benny would become the most popular star on network radio, and often credited Hoag for helping him out at a crucial moment in his life. One of Hoag's prized possessions was a signed photograph of Benny on which the performer had scribbled, "Well, Jerry, I finally got luck."[14]

JACK BENNY. BHL

But other than organ performances and an inexpensive New Year's Eve show in 1930, live shows did not appear again at the Michigan Theater until a three-day booking of Blackstone the Magician in March 1932. The elegant Harry Blackstone was an extremely popular performer throughout the 1930s and 1940s. Always in white tie and tails, Blackstone remained silent for most of his act and allowed the tricks themselves to impress the audience (one of his most effective illusions was that of a woman lying on a couch who then appeared to float into the air and vanish). Blackstone was a regular on the movie theater circuit, performing a short stage show between film screenings.

Another notable stage show at the Michigan that year was a four-day engagement in October of Fred Waring and his Pennsylvanians – a 25-member company of singers, dancers and musicians that added up to "the Costliest Stage Show ever to Play Ann Arbor," according to an *Ann Arbor Daily News* advertisement on October 7. Hoag and Waring had known each other since the 1920s, when Hoag booked Waring's band at the Majestic Theater for a week after hearing it at a U-M dance. By the early 1930s, Waring had added a chorus to his band, eventually turning his focus exclusively to choral conducting and, with the help of Robert Shaw, assembled a high-quality group of singers known as the Pennsylvanians that remained popular until the 1980s.

Vaudeville returned to the Michigan Theater in January 1933 and remained part of the Saturday-night program until July. The programs, which the theater printed in full in its newspaper ads, offer a fascinating glimpse of the range of entertainment – live acts, musical performances, and newsreels, short films, and features – presented on those Saturday nights.

The mixed program resumed in the fall of 1933 and again in the fall of 1934, but by 1935, vaudeville was essentially dead as a viable entertainment medium. Its circuits had dried up and its theaters had been converted to movie houses. Vaudeville performers such as Benny, Eddie Cantor, and George Burns and Gracie Allen moved on to network radio and soon

established themselves as stars of the new medium. And, increasingly, movie theaters that were also geared to live shows became venues for the era's popular big bands, which were becoming well known through the phenomenal growth of radio and electrical recording in the 1930s.

Starting in 1935 the Michigan Theater featured bands several times a year, often for one-night appearances. Among the ensembles that performed in 1935 were some known from their radio broadcasts, including Harry Reser and the Cliquot Club Eskimos,[15] Frank & Milt Britton's Orchestra, the Richard Humber and Ted Weems bands, Nick Lucas and his CBS Broadcasting Orchestra, and Don Bestor and his NBC Orchestra. Bestor's band was featured on the highly rated *Jack Benny Program*, broadcast on Sunday evenings over the NBC Red Network. (Benny would lead into Bestor's band with the line: "Play, Don! Play!" Bestor also wrote the famous "J-E-L-L-O" jingle for the program's sponsor.)

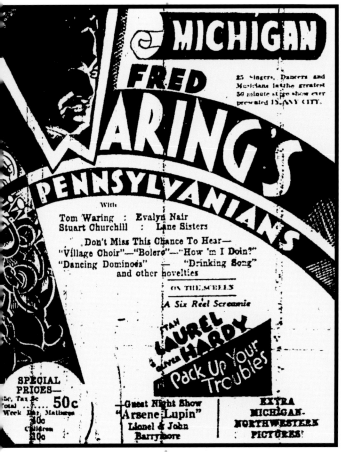

Presumably because the relatively stable U-M student population shielded it from the worst effects of the Depression, the Michigan Theater turned a fairly consistent profit in the 1930s. Hoag's account books show that the theater's typical weekly receipts were almost $4,300 and expenses totaled about $3,500 – a net of some $800 a week.

But in other parts of the state and the country, movie theaters were hit hard in the early years of the Depression. In 1932, three years after the stock market crash, film box office had dropped to approximately 50 percent of its pre-crash levels. To cut costs, theaters jettisoned expensive live shows, cut staff, and deferred maintenance. To lure audiences presenters cut ticket prices, screened double features, and developed a range of gimmicks including "Screeno," a version of bingo, and other games; Bank Night; and giveaways of everything from dishes to Thanksgiving turkeys. It was during this time that theaters introduced concession stands as another source of revenue.

It appears that the Michigan Theater did not have to resort to most of these gimmicks. However, the theater did schedule a weekly Guest Night, on which two people could attend for the price of one and, frequently, see a preview of a coming attraction – offering the ticket holder and guest two features for the price of one. The Michigan also introduced concessions in the 1930s when it set up a small candy counter in the outer lobby; popcorn and other treats were introduced later.

Still, economic forces had their impact on Michigan programming – most significantly in live performance. The resident orchestra was disbanded,[16] leaving only the organist to perform solos and accompany song slides through the 1930s. The organ was the only live portion of the silent-era program to remain constant at the Michigan Theater,[17] a tradition that continued with the hiring of Paul Tompkins in 1932.

In 1932, three years after the stock market crash, film box office had dropped to approximately 50 percent of its pre-crash levels. To cut costs, theaters jettisoned expensive live shows, cut staff, and deferred maintenance.

Weary River and its ilk aside, the 1930s are justifiably considered Hollywood's Golden Age. By the end of the decade the film industry had fully recovered from the box office slump during the early years of the Depression. Production companies were out of receivership, the art of making sound movies had been mastered and some of the decade's best-remembered films were being made.

As the principal film venue for Ann Arbor, the Michigan Theater screened some of the era's classics. The year 1936 was a fertile one for great movies, including *Mutiny on the Bounty, Rose Marie, Mr. Deeds Goes to Town,* and *My Man Godfrey.* The Michigan's offerings in 1937 and 1938 included *The Golddiggers of 1937, A Star Is Born, A Day at the Races, Jezebel,* and *The Adventures of Robin Hood.*

In the blockbuster year for movies that was 1939, the Michigan presented *Young Mr. Lincoln, Mr. Smith Goes to Washington, The Lady Vanishes, Jamaica Inn,* and *The Wizard of Oz.* Many years later, Hoag recalled standing in the lobby during a matinee screening of *Oz* when, suddenly, the doors burst open and dozens of screaming kids flooded out of the theater – spooked, apparently, by the Wicked Witch of the West's flying monkeys.

Notably, the Michigan didn't screen the biggest picture of that year; *Gone With the Wind* played at the Majestic. Jay Van Sickle of Ann Arbor recalled that he and a friend stood in the alley next to the Majestic and watched the entire three-hour, 43-minute film through a crack in the side door.

NOTES

[1] The theater's programming day, however, opened with the film half of the program, allowing one expensive stage show to entertain audiences for two feature film presentations. The same pattern – feature, stage show, feature – held for the evening performances. Radio City Music Hall followed a similar schedule for decades.

[2] Bob Howland, who took over organist duties at the Michigan in September 1928, recalled in a 1970s interview that the organist accompanied about half of the feature film and then segued into the orchestra performance for the remainder of the score. Usually the film came with a printed score, but sometimes it had to be performed without rehearsal. Howland also created his own scores (probably from existing music) and practiced them on a piano in his dressing room. Howland stayed at the Michigan Theater organ for three years, at a salary of $125 a week.

[3] Eddie Foy's family and career were immortalized in the 1950s Bob Hope film *The Seven Little Foys*; a talking film of a Foy family vaudeville routine also survives.

[4] Unlike Vitaphone, the Movietone method was portable and capable of recording sound outside the studio – clearly an advantage for newsreel production.

[5] Vitaphone and Movietone could be presented on the same amplifiers and speakers, eliminating the need to replace existing Vitaphone technology. Photophone, a somewhat superior system developed by RCA and for a time independently marketed through its RKO subsidiary, was adopted as the industry standard in 1934.

[6] Dennis M. Allen, "The Talkies Come to Ann Arbor." *Ann Arbor Observer,* November 1988.

[7] Ibid.

[8] Ibid.

[9] The film *Joy Street* was a Fox feature starring Lois Moran and Nick Stuart. Medley and Dupree headlined the stage show; the Michigan Theater Orchestra and the organist also performed.

[10] *The New York Times* critic Mordaunt Hall wrote a scathing review when the film opened at Manhattan's Central Theater in January 1929: "The chief attribute of this banal jailbird tale is that it has some interesting prison sequences, and perhaps there are those who may enthuse over Mr. Barthelmess's rendition of *Weary River*. He does sing it quite well, but it would take a far better singer and a much better song to atone for the lack of imagination and suspense in this photoplay, which is one of those that slip from silence to sound every now and again."

Ironically, it was later discovered that Barthelmess's singing voice was dubbed. And it turned out that *It's Up to You*, another of the film's featured songs that was supposedly written by Vitaphone musical director Louis Silvers, had been composed by Edward F. Craig and lifted from a 1925 Harvard Hasty Pudding show – for which Silvers had been a coach.

[11] Radio City Music Hall presented live stage shows with its movie programs until 1979.

[12] Other sound films shown during the summer of 1929 included such forgotten titles as *The Leatherneck; The Old Barn*, a short comic talkie from Mack Sennett; *The Melody of Love*, Carl Laemmle's first all-talking picture; *The Shakedown*; and *Broadway Babies*.

[13] The Michigan Union Opera began in 1908 as the all-male Mimes of the University of Michigan (or simply as "The Mimes") to raise funds for a university student union. The Mimes' first opera, *Michigenda*, was set in Ann Arbor and lampooned several U-M faculty members. The show raised $2,000 – such a success that annual productions followed, usually staged at the Whitney Theater. In 1913, the organization took its production of *Contrarie Mary* on the road to raise even more money for the Michigan Union, which was finally built in 1919. At least two other Michigan Union Opera productions were staged at the Michigan Theater after 1929's *Music-Go-Round: Froggy Bottom* in 1949 and *Film-Flam* in 1955. The group's all-male tradition ended in 1956 and it changed its name to MUSKET – Michigan Union Show, Ko-Eds Too.

[14] Norman Gibson, "Theater Manager Jerry Hoag Recalls 50 Colorful Years," *The Ann Arbor News*, October 5, 1969.

[15] Cliquot Club was a popular ginger ale; Cliquot (pronounced klee-ko) was the name of the Eskimo boy depicted in the product's advertising. The band was first heard on radio in 1923 and broadcast on New York's WEAF for three years. In 1926 it moved to NBC, where it continued off and on until the mid 1930s.

[16] Michigan Theater advertisements including mention of Karl Weiderhold and his Michigan Theater Orchestra appear up to June 1929; thereafter, the orchestra disappears from ads for the theater. The Michigan's ledger books show that theater expenses in the week following the screening of *Weary River* drop noticeably from the week before the showing of the first talking picture at the Michigan Theater.

[17] For an extended discussion of Michigan Theater's organists, the Barton Organ, and its importance to the history and character of the Michigan Theater, see Appendix C.

THE STATE THEATER MARQUEE. HBA

Wartime and the 1940s at the Michigan Theater

I N THE EARLY 1940S film exhibition in Ann Arbor entered a period of stable prosperity that would last until the end of the decade. Around the country, movie theaters saw dramatically increased attendance as the public sought war news as well as an escape from the harsh realities of the conflict. Box office receipts returned to the record levels of the late 1920s, and in 1946 hit a weekly sales peak of 96 million tickets.

Boosted by their exposure on network radio and the sale of phonograph records, big bands enjoyed especially widespread popularity as the decade began. During the first six months of 1940, for example, the Michigan hosted at least 12 popular ensembles for appearances of one or more nights. These included such groups as the Clyde Lucas Orchestra, the Buddy Rogers Orchestra, Clyde McCoy and His Orchestra, and the more familiar bands of Duke Ellington, Xavier Cugat, and Ozzie Nelson.

Programming at the Michigan Theater continued to be a mix of first-run feature films from all the major studios plus occasional stage shows, big-band appearances, and periodic road productions of opera and Broadway plays. Organist Paul Tompkins continued as a regular feature at the Michigan. The Michigan remained Ann Arbor's principal movie theater; its manager, Gerry Hoag, served as the head of all Butterfield theater operations in the city; and Butterfield continued to operate all of the movie theaters in Ann Arbor: the Michigan, Wuerth, Orpheum, Whitney – and one newcomer.[1]

THE STATE THEATER
OUTER LOBBY. HBA

The State Theater – the only Ann Arbor movie theater owned outright by Butterfield – opened on March 18, 1942, with a screening of *The Fleet's In,* a Paramount musical starring Dorothy Lamour, William Holden, Eddie Bracken, and the Jimmy Dorsey Orchestra. A newsreel and a Warner cartoon – *Rhapsody in Rivets* – were also on the program.

The Art Deco-style structure at the intersection of State and Liberty streets, just a few doors east of the Michigan, was the first new movie theater to open in Ann Arbor in 14 years. The Butterfield-operated Majestic Theater – a favorite of Ann Arbor audiences since 1907 – closed its doors and its staff was transferred to the State. The timing of the State's construction was unusual. Completed mere months after the United States entered the war, all its materials had been ordered and contracts signed in 1939 and building permits were issued on February 8, 1941. The project therefore escaped the wartime ban on civilian construction – and Butterfield widely publicized that fact to avoid criticism that it used resources vital to the war effort. The State was the last new building to go up in Ann Arbor until the end of the war, when construction materials were again available for civilian use.

The State Theater's design was heavily influenced by the Art Deco movement and its prime example, the Radio City Music Hall, which opened in 1932.

The State Theater was designed by Detroit architect C. Howard Crane. Among Crane's many other buildings was Detroit's first movie palace, the beautiful Capitol Theater, located near Grand Circus on Washington Street. Today, the Capitol has been restored and is the home of the Michigan Opera Theater. In addition, Crane designed the Fox and United Artists theaters also in Detroit as well as more than 200 theaters elsewhere.

Every effort was maade to differentiate the new State Theater from the older theaters. It was distinctly modern in design and incorporated several new technological features. The State Theater's design was heavily influenced by the Art Deco movement and its prime example, the Radio City Music Hall, which opened in 1932. The State's interiors were elegantly simple. Its walls were decorated with wainscoting and fabrics colored muted rose and green, and lit with simple wall sconces. The lobby featured recessed ceiling coves that emitted soft light, and the area was trimmed with rosewood and walnut wainscoting. Curving staircases with metal handrails led to a sweeping mezzanine and balcony area.

The State Theater seated 1,900 and therefore was slightly larger than the Michigan Theater. There was a small thrust platform directly in front of the screen that was hung close to the rear wall of the theater. There was no true stage, and even though there were pipe chambers built for it, there was no organ. The State was designed to serve exclusively as a motion picture theater. Any live acts that Butterfield might schedule would continue to appear at the Michigan.

THE STATE THEATER
MEZZANINE. HBA

The State was the first movie theater in Ann Arbor to be completely air conditioned. All other theaters, including the Michigan, were air cooled but not actually air conditioned. In fact, the State had two air conditioning systems — one for the auditorium and another for the lobby. This design allowed the temperatures in the theater itself to remain stable while the lobby doors frequently opened and closed to the outside air.

In addition, the State had the latest projectors with automatic feed systems for their carbon pencils. The theater's seats were of a sleek Art Deco design with rounded edges and plush upholstery. The seats automatically returned to upright positions when patrons stood up. The State had a centralized cleaning system that consisted of a large vacuum in the basement with hose attachments placed strategically around the building. The theater — also had a 20x26-foot perforated plastic screen. These perforations allowed sound from speakers placed behind it to flow out into the auditorium and also permitted the screen to be much lighter in construction. At the same time, the Michigan Theater also got a new screen and projectors.

Another unusual feature of the State was that it had internal fire escapes leading down from the balcony. The stairways were inside the building but sealed from the rest of the theater in such a way that patrons could exit safely in case of fire. One of those internal fire escapes now serves as the stairway to the two theaters located in the State's old balcony area.

Well before December 7, 1941, Hollywood film content was reflecting the escalating conflicts in Europe and Asia. Newsreels regularly reported on wartime activities, and Hollywood features appeared with such titles as *In the Navy, Caught in the Draft,* and *Dive Bomber.* But the Japanese attack on Pearl Harbor of course spurred a dramatic increase in war-related newsreels and film titles: the Michigan ran a Disney cartoon called *The Art of Self Defense* a month after the day that would "live in infamy," and in early February screened *The Attack on Pearl Harbor.* Capitalizing on anti-Japanese sentiment, a University of Michigan group staged a musical comedy entitled *Nips in the Bud* at the Michigan on September 30, 1943.

As well as shaping the output of the Hollywood studios, the war affected the daily operations of the Michigan Theater and movie houses like it across the country. A ring binder of memos to theater managers from E.C. Beatty – who became president of W.S. Butterfield Theatres Inc. following the death of Butterfield himself in 1936 – provides a fascinating glimpse of the period.

THE STATE THEATER
AUDITORIUM. HBA

The furnaces of many theaters in the circuit had been converted from coal to oil in the 1930s, and Butterfield sought ways to use coal again.

WARTIME SHORTAGES

The possibility that wartime shortages might force some theaters to halt operations was an immediate concern. An adequate supply of carbon rods, for example, was essential to showing films. Projectors in the 1940s used carbon arcs as high-intensity light sources. The arc was generated by sending a powerful electrical current down two carbon rods. As the electricity jumped across a small gap between the ends of the rods, it created a bright light. In the process the carbon tips burned away, and the gap between them had to be adjusted constantly. A typical projector used a pair of carbons every 30 minutes.

In anticipation of possible shortages, Beatty placed a large order in late 1939 and sent the following directive to theater operators throughout the circuit:

> We are ordering out a large consignment of carbons to each theater we operate. These carbons will not all be shipped at once but will come along in small shipments. ... The carbons being sent to your theater represent a lot of money, and we want you to place them in some special place where it is dry, under lock and key and the operators are to get these carbons, a case at a time, as they need them, from you personally. We are going to hold each manager personally responsible for the handling of carbons in this manner. You will also have to watch your operators carefully to make sure they do not waste carbons knowing there is a surplus on hand. It is possible if war continues that we may have difficulty in getting carbons at a later date, so caution your operators to conserve the supply.

As the war continued, Butterfield management also feared that a shortage of heating oil might force theaters to close during winter months. The furnaces of many theaters in the circuit had been converted from coal to oil in the 1930s, and Butterfield sought ways to use coal again. A corporate memo on May 25, 1942, outlined the problem – and reflected its urgency:

> In some instances your existing boiler can be converted to a hand-fired coal-burning job by installing grates. In some instances the boilers were converted from hand-firing with coal to oil burning or stoker fired, and the old grates which were removed may perhaps still be stored on the premises. … We cannot impress upon you too strongly how serious the situation might become and how diligently we want you to search for grates to be used for hand firing your boiler, if such an emergency arises. This problem necessitates rush action and the utmost cooperation on the part of all of you, or you may be faced with a closed theater.

Butterfield took the possibility of an actual aerial attack very seriously; Michigan, with its many manufacturing plants, was seen as particularly vulnerable. All Butterfield theater managers were required to become air raid wardens and to prepare their theaters for blackout drills. In May 1942, managers received a lengthy memo detailing their responsibilities:[2]

> In case it is necessary to evacuate the theatre, make the following announcement: "Ladies and gentlemen, due to a disturbance in the neighborhood, we have been asked by the authorities to discontinue the performance and close the theatre. There is no immediate danger; this is simply a sensible precaution we have been asked to take. Our staff are at their stations to assist you in leaving the theatre quietly and calmly. Please use the exit nearest you and take your time."

The memo also contained instructions about how to equip theaters with firehoses, sand pails, flashlights, and other emergency supplies. It ended with this admonition:

> Now, gentlemen, you have those rules and you also have this communication from the office, which by its very length should impress upon you its importance. In fact, today there is nothing more important than preparing your theatres for the protection of your patrons and property in any emergency which the war may bring.

Clearly, Butterfield management was deeply committed to supporting the war effort, and it pressured individual theater operators to persuade all employees to set aside 10 percent of their salaries for the purchase of war bonds. On July 9, 1942, Beatty wrote his managers to "go to work on those who are short of 10% at once" and offered to send "a personal letter" to those who needed prodding "if you will furnish me with their name and amount of money they are receiving each week and amount of money presently being allotted for the purchase of bonds."

Beatty also instructed managers to promote the war effort in and outside their theaters.

In a July 27 memo, Beatty noted

some hesitancy on the part of all the managers to display ... material which would be of immense aid to the government. In none of the theaters have I found sufficient war bond posters, booklets, etc. ... You will please call at your Marine Recruiting Office or any other recruiting office and see if you can get a supply of these booklets and do not hesitate to put up a poster for any of the recruiting services in your lobby if you can find an attractive one, but by all means get the proper display on the war bond and stamp sales.

The domestic requirements of wartime weren't the only concerns to appear in Beatty's interoffice communications. Memos from the period offer a look at the day-to-day operations of the Michigan and other theaters in the Butterfield circuit.

On the conduct of ushers:

Among other things ushers are selected for their attractive appearance. They will be expected to keep neat and clean.

Your uniforms are very expensive and you must take care of them. Hang them up carefully each time they are taken off. Keep them brushed, clean and mended.

Conduct yourself in a business-like manner at all times. Do not talk or joke with film-checkers. Do not slouch or lean against the wall while on duty. See that every patron coming in is offered a seat in a courteous manner.

On the appearance of theaters:

In a few of the theatres I noticed on Thanksgiving Day that the lobby had not been cleaned out between matinee and night performances. The theatre lobbies were full of waste paper and presented a very bad appearance. Will the theatres who do not follow the policy of cleaning up the paper, et cetera, between the matinee and night performances, please adopt this course in the future.[3]

On keeping to the schedule:

Be careful of intermissions. There is nothing more disturbing than to sit five or six minutes in a theatre with nothing going on. ... Now, boys,

please watch this for in a house last week which had 4 minutes' intermission multiplied by 5 (this show had 6 shows per day) took up 20 minutes of time throughout the day and the last show was out just five minutes to 12:00. This is most foolish and does nothing but cause dissatisfaction among your employees, wastes electricity and accomplishes nothing at all except the criticism from your patrons.

On messy kids:

Do you have difficulty with paper towels on Saturday afternoon or on days when you have a large juvenile attendance? In some theatres we have noticed these towels thrown all over the rest rooms, evidently by some un-thinking youngsters. In some of our theatres the managers remove the pa-per towels on Saturday afternoons. If you have this difficulty, follow the same policy.

CROWDS FOR *IT HAPPENS EVERY SPRING*. BHL

WARTIME ENTERTAINMENT AND POSTWAR FILMS

While the State was designed to serve exclusively as a motion picture theater, the Michigan Theater continued to be a principal venue for feature films and occasional stage productions throughout the war.

In January 1941, the Michigan was used to stage a road show presentation of a Broadway play. It was *Hellzapoppin*, which was a full-length musical revue featuring a company of 100 and a "Hollywood beauty chorus." The show, produced by the vaudeville team of Olsen and Johnson, had enjoyed a three-year run on Broadway and in 1942 became a feature film.

Over the next four years, a number of road show productions came to the Michigan. Most were supplied by the Schubert organization and traveled a circuit of movie theaters, including many Butterfield houses in the state of Michigan. Most played for one night only.

In January 1942, the Michigan featured a performance of the Broadway play *Separate Rooms*, with a New York cast. In 1944, there were several impressive live shows, including a production of Gershwin's *Porgy and Bess*, Verdi's *Aida*, Clarence Day's *Life with Father* (which eventually became the longest-running non-musical play on Broadway), and the Theatre Guild's production of Shakespeare's *Othello* starring Jose Ferrer, Uta Hagen, and Paul Robeson. In 1945, the theater presented Ibsen's *A Doll's House* with Francis Lederer, H.B. Warner, Dale Melbourne, and Jane Darwell.

PAUL ROBESON. BHL

Important films shown at the Michigan during the war included Walt Disney's experimental *Fantasia; King's Row*, featuring a performance by Ronald Reagan and a score by Oscar-winner Erich Korngold; Orson Welles' *Citizen Kane* and *The Magnificent Ambersons; Holiday Inn*, starring Bing Crosby and Fred Astaire and introducing Irving Berlin's classic holiday song *White Christmas; Mrs. Miniver*, which paired Walter Pidgeon and Greer Garson; *Road to Morocco*, the first of the Bing Crosby/Bob Hope "road" pictures; King Vidor's *Cabin in the Sky*, with an all African American cast; Vincente Minnelli's *Meet Me in St. Louis; National Velvet*, starring a 12-year-old Elizabeth Taylor; and *The Horn Blows at Midnight*, Jack Benny's big box office dud.

Film offerings continued to be strong in the mid- and late 1940s, with screenings of *Leave Her to Heaven*, Alfred Hitchcock's *Spellbound*, Billy Wilder's *The Lost Weekend*, Disney's *Pinocchio*, John Ford's *My Darling Clementine* and *She Wore a Yellow Ribbon*, Charles Chaplin's *Monsieur Verdoux*, David Lean's *Brief Encounter*, *Easter Parade* with Fred Astaire and Judy Garland, *Johnny Belinda*, *Adam's Rib*, *The Treasure of the Sierra Madre* and *Key Largo*, both starring Humphrey Bogart, and *The Barkleys of Broadway* – the final film teaming Fred Astaire and Ginger Rogers.

VELOZ AND YOLANDA. BHL

Stage productions continued after the war and these included a 1945 production of Verdi's *Il Trovatore*. In 1946, live performances included Xavier Cugat and his orchestra, the ballroom dancing team of Veloz and Yolanda, a stage production of *The Corn Is Green* with Ethel Barrymore, and a New Year's Eve vaudeville show. In March 1949 the Michigan Union Opera launched its production of *Froggy Bottom*, and a few weeks later jazz greats Louis Armstrong, Earl "Fatha" Hines, and Jack Teagarden appeared at the Michigan.

PAUL TOMPKINS RETURNS

The tradition of live organ music returned to the Michigan in December 1945 when Paul Tompkins returned from his Army service. Records show he was paid $50 a week for the four weeks of December, but it is unclear how often he played after his return to the theater; his name appears only occasionally in display advertisements until May 1950, but it is likely that he played on a fairly regular basis. Tompkins also began a long tenure on a Hammond organ at the Weber's Supper Club, at 3715 Jackson Road (later, the site of a car dealership) in Ann Arbor. For a month in late 1949, Tompkins' performances on the Hammond organ at Weber's were broadcast from 11:30 to midnight every evening over local radio station WHRV.

Tompkins had a featured role in a special event at the Michigan on May 12, 1949, that celebrated the release of *It Happens Every Spring*. The film was based on a short story by Shirley W. Smith, who had served for many years as an administrator at the University of Michigan. *It Happens Every Spring*, starring Ray Milland, Jean Peters, and Paul Douglas, is the story of a university professor who accidentally discovers a formula that will cause a baseball to be repelled by wood. Realizing the potential of his discovery, the professor takes a leave of absence to pitch for a St. Louis baseball team and is so successful that his team makes it to the World Series.

ETHEL BARRYMORE. BHL

THE MICHIGAN THEATER'S SECOND MARQUEE, IN 1950. BHL

Among the guests at the sold-out event, promoted as the world's first "author's premiere," were Smith; Valentine Davies, who adapted the screenplay; Ann Arbor Mayor William Brown; and other local dignitaries. A U-M band performed outside the theater; inside, the U-M Glee Club sang to the accompaniment of Tompkins on the Barton organ.

[1] When it opened the State Theater, Butterfield already controlled 114 theaters in Michigan, including 10 in Grand Rapids, eight in Flint, and seven in Lansing.

[2] The memo was striking in its detail: "It will be the duty of each manager to thoroughly organize the personnel of his theatre and mold it into a smooth-functioning theatre defense group. … Each manager should apply for and become the Chief Air Warden for his theatre and take the course. If a manager is in control of two or more theatres then the assistants in charge of the theatres should apply for and become the Chief Air Raid Wardens in those theatres and also take the Air Raid Warden Course."

[3] Beatty's advice extended to exterior maintenance as well: "Your roof should be inspected carefully at least once every three months, to see that any breaks in the roof are given immediate attention, or any evident weak spots repaired before they break through enough to cause leakage and damage. Also, all gutters and sumps around drains should be kept clear of debris and dirt, so that water will not stand on the roof or in the gutters. … You should keep a record of dates inspections are made, and calendar it at all times for future inspection dates, so that periodical inspections are not overlooked."

THE 1950s

BETWEEN 1946 AND 1952, movie attendance at U.S. theaters dropped almost 50 percent, from a high of about 100 million patrons a week in 1946 to 52 million six years later. A number of factors contributed to this decline. Men returning from military service wanted to establish families in homes of their own, fueling a suburban construction boom and separating downtown theaters from much of their audience. Young couples in the suburbs began to have children, meaning less disposable income for movie tickets and less free time for a trip downtown. Use of public transportation began to diminish and streetcar and bus services declined, but at the same time there were few parking lots in city centers to accommodate a new influx of automobiles.

A key antitrust ruling from the U.S. Supreme Court in 1948 also altered the landscape when *United States v. Paramount Pictures* forced the five large, vertically integrated film production companies to sell off their theaters. Hollywood was forced into major restructuring just as revenues were falling sharply.

Commercial television stations began to appear in major markets in 1945, and within three years more than 100 stations were broadcasting despite spotty service and an absence of television in many large cities. In 1948, the Federal Communications Commission froze approval of applications for new television stations until additional spectrum space (eventually in the UHF range) could be allocated. This moratorium ended in 1952, and soon television service became available almost everywhere. Hollywood responded to the competition by closing theaters that were no longer needed and by introducing technologies such as 3-D and widescreen to lure small-screen watchers back to movie theaters.

The Michigan hosted the National Ballet of Canada for the first time on March 20, 1957, in a program sponsored by the Ann Arbor Civic Ballet.

While these attempts largely failed and box office continued to decline throughout the decade, it appears that the Michigan and State theaters were somewhat protected from the downward slide by the constancy of the University of Michigan student population. Although their box office records from the period do not survive, the movie theaters – and the rest of the campus business district on State and Liberty streets – thrived in the 1950s. More distant from the U-M central campus, the three Butterfield theaters on Main Street continued a decline that began in the 1940s. The Orpheum and Wuerth theaters began showing second-run and foreign films; the Whitney Theater closed in 1952.

BALLET COMES TO THE MICHIGAN

The Michigan scheduled occasional live productions throughout the 1950s, including the Michigan Union Opera's last all-male production, *Film Flam*, which played for four days in December 1955.[1] Michigan Theater audiences during the decade also enjoyed performances by two important international ballet companies: Ballet Russe de Monte Carlo and the National Ballet of Canada.

In 1951, the Ballet Russe presented Tchaikovsky's *Aurora's Wedding* and scenes from *Swan Lake*, as well as excerpts from *Graduation Ball* and *Paquita*.[2] (The orchestra conductor for *Paquita* was Claude Monteux, son of famed French conductor Pierre Monteux.) In February 1952, the company returned to a full house at the Michigan for a single-evening performance that included scenes from Offenbach's *Gaite Parisienne*, a setting of Rimsky-Korsakoff's *Capriccio Espagnole*, the "Bluebird" pas de deux from *Aurora's Wedding*, *Les Sylphides*, and a reprise of *Graduation Ball*, performed the year before.[3]

The Michigan hosted the National Ballet of Canada for the first time on March 20, 1957, in a program sponsored by the Ann Arbor Civic Ballet. The program featured *Les Rendezvous*, a ballet that had been in the repertoire of London's Sadler's Wells Ballet company, and *Orpheus in the Underworld*, to music by Jacques Offenbach. The final number was a contemporary production called *Postscript* that was choreographed to jazz – and did not please *Ann Arbor News* reviewer Lola Gehring. In an otherwise positive review of the evening, she called *Postscript* "a disappointment" whose "spirited performances by Sylvia Mason and Robert Ito failed to make up for the ballet's inherent weaknesses. 'Postscript'… is essentially a dance for musical comedy and as such has … no place in the repertoire of a ballet company."[4]

The National Ballet of Canada appeared at the Michigan a second time on February 10, 1958, again sponsored by the Ann Arbor Civic Ballet. The program included *Winter Night*, set to Rachmaninoff's Piano Concerto No. 2.

A 1951 PROGRAMME. MT

WIDESCREEN

Hollywood introduced several technological improvements in the 1950s – including widescreen, 3-D, stereophonic sound, and greater use of color photography – to add dazzle to the viewing experience not to be found on the television screen.

Cinerama, the first widescreen system introduced by the industry, utilized three interlocked cameras to record a very wide image and a fourth to record a multitrack soundtrack on 35-millimeter film. Selected theaters around the country, including the Wilson Theater in Detroit, were reconfigured to accommodate the deeply curved screen and the additional projectors required.[5] A more practical widescreen technology was the anamorphic process that squeezed a wide image onto standard 35-millimeter film by means of a special lens. An identical lens attached to the front of the

projector "unsqueezed" the image on a wide screen. This approach, introduced by 20th Century Fox as Cinemascope in 1953, became the dominant widescreen system within a few years.

The State Theater installed a Cinemascope screen in November 1953. It was 43 feet wide and 24 feet high and was covered with highly reflective particles embedded in the plastic material of the screen. The process – known as "Miracle Mirror" – increased the brightness of the widescreen image (and would do the same for 3-D projection). The new screen at the State was first used for the standard-size *All the Brothers Were Valiant*. The first widescreen film shown at the State was *The Robe*, which opened on Thanksgiving Day. (The Biblical epic, starring Richard Burton and Jean Simmons, was based on a popular novel written by Lloyd C. Douglas – one-time pastor of the First Congregational Church in Ann Arbor.)

For most of 1954, the State (with a screen 7 feet wider than that at the Michigan) was the favored venue for widescreen films in Ann Arbor and presented such memorable releases as *How To Marry a Millionaire*, starring Marilyn Monroe and Jane Russell; *Beneath the 12-Mile Reef*, with a musical score by Bernard Herrmann; MGM's first widescreen film, *Knights of the Round Table* with Robert Taylor; *Prince Valiant; River of No Return,* also with Marilyn Monroe; *Three Coins in the Fountain; The High and the Mighty;* and *Demetrius and the Gladiators,* a sequel to *The Robe.*

With Paramount's *White Christmas*[6] in November 1954, the Michigan began to show widescreen films on its slightly smaller screen using the VistaVision process. The VistaVision system achieved a wide image by exposing 35-millimeter film as it ran sideways, rather than vertically, through the camera. This allowed the camera to record more visual information on a wider area of film while still using standard 35-millimeter film stock. The exposed film was then processed and each frame was reduced in size to fit into the frame format of standard, vertically threaded projectors that were equipped with special lenses that could project the higher-resolution image onto a wider screen. By developing its own system, Paramount avoided the humiliating prospect of leasing the anamorphic system from its competitor 20th Century Fox.

The Michigan was the first venue in Ann Arbor to project 3-D features. The first, *Bwana Devil,* premiered April 9, 1953; *House of Wax* arrived the following month; and *Fort Ti* and *It Came From Outer Space* were screened in June. The illusion of depth necessary for the 3-D image could be achieved by recording images slightly displaced horizontally from one another, using two separate cameras. In screening the film, two interlocked projectors used polarizing filters set at 90 degrees to one another to place the images on the screen. Viewers wore glasses with polarizing lenses that allowed the left eye to see one of the images and the right eye to see the other. The need for two separate cameras and two projectors meant this process was expensive, so the studios also released some 3-D films created by an "anaglyph" process, which used red and blue filters to accomplish the illusion but placed both images on a single strip of film.

DONNA REED AND
JOHN DEREK. BHL

The anaglyph process eliminated the need for two projectors operating simultaneously and thus significantly reduced costs and technical difficulties, but produced a less convincing 3-D illusion.

The public fascination with the gimmick, produced by either process, was short lived. By the time *Creature From the Black Lagoon* and *Dial M for Murder* were screened at the Michigan Theater in February and May 1954, they were shown "flat" rather than in 3-D.

Despite the continued drop in the box office in the early 1950s, Hollywood released a number of impressive films. Some of the major releases to play at the Michigan included *High Noon, Ivanhoe, The Snows of Kilimanjaro, From Here to Eternity, Roman Holiday, Peter Pan, Shane, The Bandwagon, Moulin Rouge,* and *The Country Girl.*

A less noteworthy film screened at the Michigan produced an opportunity for a visit from Hollywood stars Donna Reed and John Derek in 1951. Opening amid the Michigan Wolverines' gridiron season, Columbia Pictures' *Saturday's Hero* gave "the lowdown on the 'kept men' of big-time college football!"[7] (Wisconsin Sen. J. William Fulbright weighed in, too: "A graphic portrayal of shocking practices as I know them.") Reed (*It's a*

The Michigan's ornate splendor seemed dated and old fashioned to 1950s tastes, which were turning to a more sleek and "modern" look.

Wonderful Life, From Here to Eternity) and Derek (better known later as husband of *10* star Bo Derek) appeared on the Michigan's stage briefly before both screenings on Saturday, September 29. Personal appearances by stars at movie houses were rare by the 1950s, and this is the only one recorded for the Michigan during its years as a commercial motion picture theater.

A NEW LOOK AND A NEW THEATER

At mid-decade, Ann Arbor would begin to see a series of dramatic changes in its movie theater operations that were due to the continuing nationwide box office slump. The first of these occurred during the summer of 1956, when Butterfield remodeled the Michigan Theater.

The Michigan's ornate splendor seemed dated and old fashioned to 1950s tastes, which were turning to a more sleek and "modern" look. The rectangular 1940s marquee was replaced with a simple triangular version, and a red, street-level box office was installed. Inside, the ceiling and walls of the outer lobby were covered with a dropped ceiling and mirrors. The sconces, chandeliers, and mirrors were removed from the grand foyer and its walls were painted in a blue and coral scheme. In the auditorium itself, the elaborate organ grills were replaced by simple arches and the multicolored paint scheme made to conform to the lobby's quieter tones. The theater was recarpeted, restrooms were updated, and air conditioning was installed in the outer lobby. The new look of the theater, which never closed during the remodeling, was unveiled on September 26, 1956. In an *Ann Arbor News* advertisement for the grand opening, manager Gerry Hoag boasted that patrons would "step into a new era of the entertainment world."[8]

Big changes in theater operations continued in early 1957. Butterfield closed the last movie theaters on Main Street – the Orpheum and the Wuerth – on March 10. The Orpheum's final film was the vintage classic *Mutiny On the Bounty*; the Wuerth ended its run with 1954's *The Member of the Wedding*. Both theaters had been marginal operations for several years, although the Orpheum had established something of a reputation for running foreign films. A week after the closings, Butterfield opened the Campus Theater on South University Avenue (later a two-story retail space that housed Tower Records and McDonald's) in the heart of the student business district.

A display ad for the opening of the Campus Theater heralded "a new era of motion picture entertainment in the Ann Arbor area."[9] It was described as "intimate … cheerful … restful … built to present the greater motion pictures of today at their very best . . . both audibly and visually. Spic and span in its new dress to give you comfort and enjoyment." The Campus Theater had a long and narrow auditorium that seated about 1,100 people. The lobby was just large enough to hold a concession stand and waiting patrons. The plain façade consisted of glass and aluminum doors across the entire width of the entrance; the triangular marquee was similar

to the one newly installed at the Michigan. In fact, the marquee, doors, carpet, lighting fixtures, and other trim at the Campus were virtually identical to those at the Michigan. It was probably while designing the Campus that Butterfield decided to remodel the Michigan; the company merely purchased more of the fixtures planned for the new theater and used them in reappointing the older one.

The Campus Theater quickly made a name for itself as a worthy successor to the Orpheum by running a series of high-quality foreign and American films. Its first feature was Vincente Minnelli's *Lust for Life*, with Kirk Douglas as Vincent van Gogh. In the months that followed, it also screened Tyrone Guthrie's *Oedipus Rex*, Federico Fellini's *La Strada*, and Akira Kurosawa's *Seven Samurai*.

THE CAMPUS THEATER
LOBBY. BHL

CENSORED AT THE CAMPUS THEATER

Since the early 1950s films had become notably more challenging in their content, and American theaters were beginning to screen films with more mature subject matter. The Production Code censorship system in place since the early 1930s was collapsing, its demise hastened by a landmark 1952 Supreme Court ruling that extended First Amendment protections to film.[10] "The Miracle Case" ruling freed theater operators to show films with more explicit sexual content, and the Campus soon became known for racy and suggestive fare.

For three weeks in February 1958 the Campus screened Roger Vadim's film *And God Created Woman*, a picture that made Brigitte Bardot an overnight sensation and pushed the boundaries of acceptable nudity in American cinema. Even though the print shown in America was heavily edited, the film still contained enough nudity to attract the attention of concerned parents and pressure groups across the country. Advertisements for the film proclaimed it to be "much more than American audiences are used to seeing of what 23-year-old girls are made of. And God created woman, but the devil invented Brigitte Bardot." The film was condemned by the Catholic Legion of Decency.

And God Created Woman made some local residents nervous. "We had the misfortune of seeing the previews," one reader wrote in *The Ann Arbor News*,

> and if your readers could have seen the faces in that Campus Theater audience, you would have cringed at the reactions. As Miss Bardot slithered through "the mud" to a final insult, her innocent brown eyes peering at us through a wedding veil, I felt somehow that I must be at fault. I am a member of the mass audience the movie kings market their putrid sextravaganzas for. ... The responsibility of theater owners and managers seems apparent, but more important is our responsibility as citizens. Some of us protested when the thumb-sucking heroine of "Baby Doll" graced our local screens, but there were not enough indignant individuals who stood against such movies being shown or else we wouldn't be faced with this Brigot [*sic*] insult.[11]

Butterfield management apparently took notice of such criticism. On February 22, the organization ran a display ad in *The Ann Arbor News* touting 10 films "that speak for themselves" scheduled for upcoming screenings at the Michigan and State, including *The Bridge on the River Kwai, Raintree County, A Farewell to Arms, The Brothers Karamazov,* and *Run Silent, Run Deep.*

In the immediate wake of the controversy over *And God Created Woman,* Butterfield took the unusual step of actually censoring a film at the Campus Theater. *The Time of Desire* opened on Thursday, February 27, 1958. The 1957 production, while not particularly memorable (*The New York Times* called it "a tepid, clumsily handled bore for the most part"), suggested a lesbian relationship between two 19th-century sisters and contained a nude scene in a lake that prompted a village busybody to label them as "odd."

According to a short article in *The Ann Arbor News* on February 28, the film was pulled and *How to Murder a Rich Uncle,* with Charles Coburn and Wendy Hiller, was substituted: "The replaced movie, which ran last night only, was deemed by Butterfield Theaters Inc. officials as not suitable for Ann Arbor audiences."

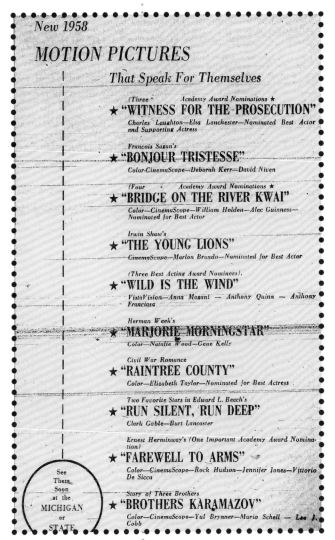

New 1958

MOTION PICTURES

That Speak For Themselves

(Three   Academy Award Nominations ★
★ "WITNESS FOR THE PROSECUTION"
Charles Laughton—Elsa Lanchester—Nominated Best Actor
and Supporting Actress

Francois Sagan's
★ "BONJOUR TRISTESSE"
Color-CinemaScope—Deborah Kerr—David Niven

(Four   Academy Award Nominations ★
★ "BRIDGE ON THE RIVER KWAI"
Color—CinemaScope—William Holden—Alec Guinness—
Nominated for Best Actor

Irwin Shaw's
★ "THE YOUNG LIONS"
CinemaScope—Marlon Brando—Nominated for Best Actor

(Three Best Acting Award Nominees).
★ "WILD IS THE WIND"
VistaVision—Anna Magani — Anthony Quinn — Anthony
Franciasa

Herman Week's
★ "MARJORIE MORNINGSTAR"
Color—Natalie Wood—Gene Kelly

Civil War Romance
★ "RAINTREE COUNTY"
Color—Elizabeth Taylor—Nominated for Best Actress

Two Favorite Stars in Edward L. Beach's
★ "RUN SILENT, RUN DEEP"
Clark Gable—Burt Lancaster

Ernest Hemingway's (One Important Academy Award Nomina-
tion)
★ "FAREWELL TO ARMS"
Color—CinemaScope—Rock Hudson—Jennifer Jones—Vittorio
De Sicca

Story of Three Brothers
★ "BROTHERS KARAMAZOV"
Color—CinemaScope—Yul Brynner—Mario Schell — Lee J.
Cobb

See
Them
Soon
at the
MICHIGAN
or
STATE

Although surviving documents do not reveal who made the decision to pull the film, it is possible that the action was taken by Gerry Hoag himself, as house manager for the Michigan Theater and city manager for all of Ann Arbor's Butterfield theaters. Hoag might have been called over to the Campus Theater after the first screening and decided to pull *The Time of Desire* after viewing the second showing.

The cancellation provoked an intense response, both for and against Butterfield's decision. A letter published in *The Ann Arbor News* called it "a most offensive instance of unilateral censorship. ... Butterfield Enterprises ought to get off their pedestal of public morality, where they are embarrassingly placed, and allow the citizens of Ann Arbor to pay their 90 cents and make their own moral decisions."[12]

In an editorial on March 3, *The Michigan Daily* took a broader view: "The important point ... is not that we have been prevented from seeing *The Time of Desire* locally, but that this incident is just one more symptom of a current widespread trend toward censorship of public reading and entertainment."[13]

The Washtenaw Council of Churches wrote Butterfield in support on March 12: "We would like to have our community feel that they can attend a movie, or let their young people attend, without being exposed to the wrong type of presentation. It is our hope that the offerings at the Butterfield Theatres in Ann Arbor will reflect this type of approach." Another Hoag supporter wrote simply to "compliment you for the good sense you showed by replacing the movie that was scheduled at the Campus Theater."

On balance, however, the respondents were opposed to the Butterfield action. This letter to Butterfield is an overall representation of their position:

Whether this decision was your own, or the influence of some local group(s) bent on censoring our movies, makes little difference to me. I just don't like it. If a picture is immoral, brutal, sadistic, trashy or just in poor taste, I prefer to be the one who decides whether or not to pay 90 cents to see it. This action on your part may well lose more patrons for you than if you stuck to democratic principles and showed the original movie.[14]

This incident illustrated the increasing difficulty faced by theater managers as the times changed – feeling responsible on one hand to uphold public morality and on the other to present interesting, stimulating films. Another letter to *The Ann Arbor News* offered

some words of support for the liberal policy being followed by the management of the Campus Theater. I believe that such a theater is filling an important need in this university community and that, with very few if any exceptions, its offerings have been of stimulating, constructive content and thought-provoking as well as entertaining … We here in Ann Arbor need to experience a variety and depth of ideas in film experience just as we need to be knowledgeable in a variety and depth of ideas in experience in books and … in plays that are staged here.[15]

The censorship of *The Time of Desire* is the only recorded instance of a film being pulled by Butterfield. Troubled though he frequently was by the increasingly liberal content of films, there is no evidence that Hoag again permitted a film to be canceled at an Ann Arbor Butterfield theater.

NOTES

[1] *Film Flam*, tellingly, played off contemporary Hollywood's trend toward technologies that produced a more spectacular viewing experience. "The thin plot," wrote a reviewer from *The Ann Arbor News*, "concerns a dying motion picture company, Passe Studios, which faces extinction because it hasn't come up with something of its own akin to 'Cinerama,' 'Feelerama' or 'Colorama.'" The show's characters included "Milly B. DeCecil" and "Clark Garble."

[2] Ballet Russe de Monte Carlo was founded by Rene Blum and Vassily de Basil in 1933 as a successor to Sergei Diaghilev's Ballets Russes. The company performed throughout the United States and introduced the art form to many American communities.

[3] A number of misfortunes to befall the cast forced some last-minute program changes: Lead dancer Frederick Franklin suffered a serious knee injury during rehearsals and several other members of the cast became ill; principal dancer Gertrude Tyven had to cancel because of her father's sudden death. Despite the problems, *The Ann Arbor News* gave the production a glowing review.

[4] *The Ann Arbor News*, March 21, 1957.

[5] Later renamed The Music Hall, the Wilson Theater was remodeled in 1952 to accommodate Cinerama.

[6] *White Christmas* was a postwar reworking of *Holiday Inn;* both films starred Bing Crosby and featured the classic Irving Berlin song.

[7] The entry for *Saturday's Hero* in *The New York Times All Movie Guide* reads: "John Derek plays a Polish-American immigrant who excels in high school sports. Though no great shakes academically, Derek wins a scholarship at an exclusive Southern university. Sidney Blackmer is a wealthy alumnus who sees to it that Derek is allowed to coast in his classes so that he can play football — and help Blackmer win a series of lucrative wagers on the games. When Derek is sidelined by an injury, Blackmer loses interest, but the rich man's niece (Donna Reed) remains faithful to the boy. The old business of subsidizing (and exploiting) college athletes is given a critical scrutiny … though the film ends happily with Derek bearing down on his classroom work and making something out of himself without relying on football."

[8] *The Ann Arbor News,* September 26, 1956.

[9] *The Ann Arbor News,* March 16, 1957.

[10] In its ruling in *Joseph Burstyn Inc. v. Wilson,* involving Roberto Rosellini's film *The Miracle,* the U.S. Supreme Court overturned a 1915 ruling under which film was treated as a business and instead defined it as an art form with free-speech protections.

[11] *The Ann Arbor News,* February 25, 1958.

[12] "Criticizes Theater Action in Withdrawing Picture," letter from Curtis E. Rodgers, *The Ann Arbor News,* March 4, 1958.

[13] *The Michigan Daily* editorial was titled "The Problem of Censorship": "The immediate case – cancellation of "Time of Desire" at the Campus Theatre this week – is insignificant in itself. The movie may actually be as unwholesome as one Butterfield Theatres Inc. vice president apparently feels it is. … That the local incident was the decision of the vice president of the theatre chain, and not the result of any 'anti-obscenity' campaign is heartening. It is, however, rather difficult to believe that any theatre management would cancel a potentially very profitable movie engagement without the application of some considerable external pressure. The Butterfield management nevertheless denies that the decision was prompted by any such pressure."

[14] Letter, dated February 28, 1958, from Edward Marcus to W.S. Butterfield Theatres Inc. Gerald H. Hoag Papers, Box 1, University of Michigan, Bentley Historical Library.

[15] *The Ann Arbor News,* February 28, 1958.

CHAPTER 6

THE END OF AN ERA: 1960s AND 1970s

EVERY DECADE in the history of the Michigan Theater brought changes, but none were more dramatic than those that occurred during its last 20 years as a commercial motion picture house.

When the 1960s began, the traditional Hollywood studio system was almost at an end. By the end of the 1970s, it was completely gone. Films still bore the logos of Paramount and MGM, but they were no longer actually being made in the production facilities of these studios. Instead, films were independent productions that might be financed in part by the big studios and probably distributed by them, but otherwise not connected to these organizations.

By the mid-1960s the studio selloff of its theaters was complete and, as a result of this divestiture and declining box office, hundreds of palatial downtown theaters had closed. In their place, movie exhibition companies were building shopping-mall cinemas with multiple screens, small auditoriums, stripped-down designs, and oversized concession stands. By the end of the 1970s, these would be the principal venues for almost all commercial films.

OPPOSITE: THE WAYSIDE
THEATER. BHL

the name selected for the new art cinema theatre

From the thousands of entries in the "Theatre Without A Name" contest, "Vth Forum" has been selected as the best name for the new theatre. The free tickets for the first 300 people to enter the contest will be in the mail soon. These tickets are good for any show, except opening night, during the first month the theatre is open.

First Prize, an all-expense paid trip for two to Bermuda, goes to T. Kennedy for his suggestion of the winning name.

Second Prize of $50 goes to Bob Forman.

Third Prize of $25 goes to Reade Pierce.

grand opening friday, dec. 9

210 South Fifth Avenue
761-9700

The 1960s saw a dramatic cultural shift, propelled by the civil rights movement, the unpopular Vietnam War, and the assassinations of President John F. Kennedy, the Rev. Dr. Martin Luther King Jr., and Sen. Robert F. Kennedy. Campus protests, street marches, newly open and wider experimentation with drugs, emerging feminism, and the change in sexual relationships brought about in large part by the introduction of the birth control pill all contributed to the transformation of American films and their audiences. Then, in 1968, the Motion Picture Association of America instituted a ratings system (still in use today) that replaced the 1930s-era Production Code; what was essentially the role of censor shifted from the producer of films to the exhibitor.

The presence of a large student population on the University of Michigan campus – just a few blocks from the Michigan Theater – continued to cushion the theater from much of the economic impact of social and industry changes. While in most communities, downtown movie theaters were a thing of the past as the 1960s began, the Michigan, State, and Campus theaters continued to be reasonably profitable. Still, these shifts were apparent to the manager of the Michigan.

In November 1960, Gerry Hoag shared his observations in a letter to M.F. Gowthorpe, president of W.S. Butterfield Theatres Inc.:

> The severe decline in local theatre attendance is most disturbing, and is perhaps due to factors beyond our control. This letter is not intended to provide an alibi.

> But as I am in my lobby every night, one thing has been observed. Previously when we emptied a crowd, large or small, they went out in large part discussing what they had seen. They might be panning, praising, picking out some particular scene or star, or maybe even extolling the music or the color. But they exited talking about the movie.

The presence of a large student population on the University of Michigan campus—just a few blocks from the Michigan Theater—continued to cushion the theater from much of the economic impact of social and industry changes.

But of late, too many times they go out talking about anything and everything but the show. And after months of this observation, it has become obvious that these folks are embarrassed and are avoiding discussing the picture or its content.

I write this fact which I admit to no one outside, because I am fully aware that only a person in your position may make a comment that will carry any weight with those responsible for our screen fare.

Maybe we can't go back to "Thin Man" or "Andy Hardy" days, but we must find a happier medium than what has been provided by the puerile minds who have tried to copy Tennessee Williams.[1]

It is likely that Hoag was reacting to the gradual liberalization of screen content that had been taking place since the 1950s. Although the Michigan ran a few provocative films in the early 1960s, such as *Suddenly, Last Summer; The Dark at the Top of the Stairs;* and *Lolita,* its films remained for the most part those that appealed to traditional tastes: *Inherit the Wind, The Parent Trap, Breakfast at Tiffany's, The Music Man.*

But Hoag also might have been expressing frustration with changing film exhibition practices. Distributors had started imposing extended runs, forcing the theater to lengthen its screening schedules from an average of four days per film to a minimum of seven. Beginning with *Charade* in January 1964, films would remain at the Michigan for as long as three weeks (*The Sound of Music* ran for eight weeks in 1967, *Funny Girl* for six in 1969). The number of films booked per year dropped from an average of 100-plus in the 1930s to more than 50 in the 1950s – and to 25 to 30 in

the 1960s. The number dwindled further as the Michigan moved into the 1970s; as attendance declined, popular and prestigious films went to other theaters and runs increased in length, the number of films that appeared at the Michigan dropped to under 20.

One important film to play at the Michigan in these years was Alfred Hitchcock's *Psycho*, which came to the theater on August 5, 1960. In addition to its classic shower scene that challenged Hollywood's squeamishness about both screen nudity and graphic violence, *Psycho* was on the cutting edge in changing in film exhibition practices.

Theaters had long been accustomed to screening films on a continuous basis throughout the day. A patron could purchase a ticket at any time, enter the theater at any point in the film's screening and keep the seat as long as he or she wanted. As often as not, movie viewers would leave when the film reached the point "where we came in." But Hitchcock insisted that audiences see *Psycho* from the very beginning and that no patron be allowed to enter the theater once the film had started. "By the way, after you see the picture, please don't give away the ending," the Hitchcockian display ad read. "It's the only one we have." This practice was ultimately adopted for all films. Today, patrons buy tickets for a particular screening and vacate the theater when that showing is over.

Other notable films to receive their Ann Arbor premieres at the Michigan in the 1960s were *To Kill a Mockingbird*, *Dr. No*, *Tom Jones*, *Dr. Strangelove*, *From Russia With Love*, *Mary Poppins*, *Dr. Zhivago*, *Barefoot in the Park*, and a flat version of the last three-panel Cinerama feature, *How the West Was Won*.[2]

The 1960s saw the end of live stage productions presented while the Michigan was still a first-run movie theater. The Ann Arbor Western Kiwanis Club sponsored *Vaude-Capades of 1961* in February; in December, the theater presented Tyrone Guthrie's production of Gilbert and Sullivan's

The Pirates of Penzance. The show, with a live orchestra and a cast of 50, was enthusiastically reviewed in *The Ann Arbor News:* The production was "like a liquor-filled bon-bon," the reviewer wrote, "first the chocolate melts, then the tongue begins to tingle, and then the fun begins."[3] In February 1962, the Kiwanis offered a second *Vaude-Capades* that included longtime house organist Paul Tompkins.[4] But Tompkins played a Gulbransen electronic organ while the great Barton pipe organ languished, silent, in the orchestra pit. Perhaps by this time the Barton, which had not been used regularly since 1950, was in need of repair.

On April 30, 1963, the Michigan Theater presented a staging of Edward Albee's *Who's Afraid of Virginia Woolf?* It was one of several plays offered during the first season of the University of Michigan's Professional Theatre Program and the only one performed at the Michigan, and had been sold out weeks in advance.[5]

The production won favorable reviews and also pleased producer Richard Barr, who told *The Ann Arbor News* that the "skeleton set" designed for the Ann Arbor performance was closer to his original concept than was the play's Broadway set. "In New York I was overruled," Barr said. *The News* reported that "the theatrical resources of Ann Arbor" also drew praise from lead actress Kate Reid: "When I learned we'd been sold out for a month," she said, "well – this is the kind of audience an actress has pleasant dreams about."[6]

Even the Michigan's backstage facilities won kudos from the company. In a note to Hoag, Robert C. Schnitzer, executive director of the U-M Professional Theatre Program, wrote, "It should especially be noted that the members of the cast were pleasantly surprised to find their dressing rooms in as good condition as they would in a Broadway house. Every one of them mentioned his appreciation of the accommodations."[7]

Schnitzer concluded his note with the hope that "this is the first of many profitable and successful collaborations for us." However,

The 556-seat Fifth Forum was designed by local architect Lester Fader, an associate professor of architecture in the U-M Department of Architecture and Design.

it turns out that the Michigan Theater was never again used as a venue for a U-M PTP presentation – perhaps because the opening of the Power Center for the Performing Arts in 1966 rendered the Michigan unnecessary. In any case, after the lights when down on *Who's Afraid of Virginia Woolf?* the Michigan Theater stage would not be used again for 14 years.[8]

NEW MOVIE THEATERS IN ANN ARBOR

The Michigan faced new competition when three new theaters opened in the Ann Arbor area between 1966 and 1970. The first of these was the Fifth Forum,[9] at 210 South Fifth Street, which opened on December 7, 1966, with a screening of Jean-Luc Godard's *A Married Woman*. Fifth Forum was billed as a "new cinema art theatre" that would "offer award-winning films from the European film festivals as well as domestic films of artistic value." The company's president, Roger Robinson, said Fifth Forum "was designed to act as a showcase for films of quality and artistic interest. It will present the finest and most unique film fare available in the United States and foreign markets."[10]

The 556-seat Fifth Forum was designed by local architect Lester Fader, an associate professor of architecture in the U-M Department of Architecture and Design. It included lounges, and on a second floor patrons could enjoy coffee and view paintings and sculpture while waiting to enter the auditorium. Fader said that the design theme for the building was "simple elegance" intended to combine old and new theater characteristics to best accent "the art of the new cinema." "The film is of primary importance [and] the building was constructed with this in mind," he said.[11]

The Fox Village Theater opened at 375 North Maple Road (later the site of Plum Market) in the Maple Village Shopping Center on July 12,

1967, with a showing of *The Dirty Dozen.* The first of Ann Arbor's mall theaters was a 957-seat cinderblock building designed by Drew Eberson (son of John Eberson, a renowned architect of grand movie palaces in the 1920s) for Fox Eastern, a subsidiary of National General Corp. The project cost a modest $500,000 and the location offered plenty of free parking. The grand opening was celebrated with an appearance by TV and western film actor Chill Wills (also known as the voice of Francis the Talking Mule).

Not to be outdone by new competition, Butterfield opened the Wayside Theater on January 12, 1968 (the first show was the forgettable *Fitzwilly,* starring Dick Van Dyke and Barbara Feldon). Located at 3020 Washtenaw Avenue in a shopping mall halfway between Ann Arbor and Ypsilanti, the theater was designed by Louis Wiltse and seated just over 1,000 people. It had what was then one of the largest theater screens in the country and could be expanded from a standard aperture (43 feet by 26 feet) to 56 feet by 24 feet for Cinemascope presentations (the mattes could be adjusted by remote controls in the projection booth). The theater had a sloped floor, sound-absorbing ceiling tiles, and acoustical blocks along the back wall. The lobby was designed to look like a comfortable living room with sofas, chairs, end tables with lamps, paintings on the walls, and a color scheme of muted browns, yellows, and tangerine. Display ads indicated Butterfield was anxious to promote the Wayside as a truly modern theater equal to any that competitors might build on the outskirts of Ann Arbor.

THE DECLINE OF THE MICHIGAN

In 1970, the Michigan Theater entered its final decade as a first-run, commercial motion picture theater. It faced a declining audience, a decreasing number of strong films and intense competition from additional screens and new theaters.

In the early 1970s, the Michigan Theater was still the flagship of Butterfield's Ann Arbor fleet, which also included the State, Campus, Wayside,

THE MODERNIZED OUTER
LOBBY. MT

and University Drive-In (located at the present site of Ann Arbor 20+ IMAX theaters). The Fifth Forum and Fox Village theaters brought the total number of Ann Arbor movie screens to seven. In 1972, the Movies at Briarwood Mall added another four screens.

Despite the added competition, Butterfield was able to attract some good films to its downtown theaters. It was aided in doing so by a process called "splitting," a strategy adopted by exhibitors in Ann Arbor and many other cities to weaken the ability of film distributors to exact exorbitant box office guarantees from individual theaters. Local managers would meet periodically, screen available films (or at least read detailed descriptions), and assign films to theaters. In this way, a distributor could not force a theater to pay an excessively high fee for any one film since the theaters were not actually bidding against one another.

GERRY HOAG IN THE
TICKET OFFICE. BHL

As city manager for Butterfield, Hoag could always make sure his beloved Michigan Theater got many of the best available films. Between 1970 and 1972, the Michigan screened such important films as *The Reivers*, based on William Faulkner's final novel; *They Shoot Horses, Don't They?*; *Airport*; *Catch-22*; *Love Story*; *Ryan's Daughter*; *Summer of '42*; *Straw Dogs*; and *The Godfather*, which had an unprecedented run of more than two months. There were other hits in the 1970s as well: In 1974, *That's Entertainment* and *Chinatown* enjoyed long runs. The strongest film in 1975 was *Three Days of the Condor*; it ran for two months. In 1976, only *That's Entertainment, Part II* and *Marathon Man* were outstanding hits.

As the decade progressed, the quality of films continued to decline; for every *Sounder*, *Sleuth*, or *The Day of the Jackal* there were films like *The Outfit*, *Jonathan Livingston Seagull*, and *Harry In Your Pocket*. With fewer good films and more screens in town, it was getting harder for the Michigan to get good product, and sometimes it screened such forgettable films as *Pardon My Blooper* and *The Magic of the Kite*. In 1978 and 1979, only

Competitive bidding put the Michigan at a particular disadvantage because it often had to put up large cash guarantees and promise long runs in order to get particular films.

Same Time, Next Year was able to bring in large crowds;[12] it was the Michigan's last successful film in its life as a commercial theater.

In 1977, the practice of splitting was ruled illegal under antitrust regulations. In 1978, Fox Village joined the ranks of the multiplexes, dividing its one large theater and adding two new screens, bringing its total to four. The Michigan found itself bidding against Movies at Briarwood, Fox Village, and other theaters for individual films, and the best product commonly went to the multiplexes. The change in the Michigan Theater's status became vividly clear in the summer of 1977, when *Star Wars* opened at the Briarwood theaters to huge crowds while the Michigan screened *Orca: The Killer Whale* and *The Bad News Bears in Breaking Training* for, needless to say, small audiences.

Competitive bidding put the Michigan at a particular disadvantage because it often had to put up large cash guarantees and promise long runs in order to get particular films. Because the theater was so large, the film could run through its potential audience very quickly; but the theater was obliged to continue screening it for the length of the promised run and the film could end up playing to virtually empty houses for weeks. This happened in December 1978 when the Michigan put up a guarantee of $100,000 for *The Wiz* and promised a run of several weeks. After a strong opening weekend, the crowds thinned dramatically.

Adding to the revenue pressures were operating costs. The multiplexes could show several films to the Michigan's one and required no additional staff; one projectionist could handle the several screens, and a ticket taker plus a few concession workers could operate the entire theater. In addition, the smaller theaters were easier to heat, cool, and keep clean. The aging Michigan was getting expensive to operate.[13]

The theater's physical decline was evident. Built in 1928, its remodeling was two decades in the past. In September 1970, Butterfield's theater inspector noted 12 cleanliness violations at the theater. None were serious, but Hoag was advised to hire extra help to address the problems.[14] Patrons weighed in, too; in September 1970 a customer wrote to complain

> about the very sloppy showing of [Tell Me That You Love Me,] Junie
> Moon on Saturday, Sept. 26 at the 5 p.m. show. ... [T]he movie was out
> of focus and we were told that there was nobody there that knew how to
> adjust the film and to be patient, for the reels would change every 20 min-
> utes. ... [H]alfway thru the movie the film reels were mixed up and the
> movie jumped to the ending of the story and then back to the part that
> we had missed. What a mess! ... [A]t the last half hour of the movie your
> concession-stand girls opened the main doors to the lobby and stood there
> laughing and talking so loud that we couldn't even hear the movie. We po-
> litely asked the girls to quiet down so we could hear. They laughed and shut
> one of the doors. (P.S. In my 32 years of living in Ann Arbor I know this set
> of circumstances is not the usual policy of the Michigan Theater.)[15]

Hoag responded with an apology for "our horrible operation of my beloved Michigan Theater," writing that the complaint "elicited definite action. ... I sincerely hope that the replacement of the personnel involved will prove more reliable."[16]

HOAG RETIRES

Gerry Hoag ended a remarkable 50-year career with Butterfield Theatres when he retired on January 5, 1974.

He was replaced by Frederick G. Caryl, the 26-year-old manager of the State Theater. Caryl began his career at Butterfield in 1964 as an usher

Gerry Hoag ended a remarkable 50-year career with Butterfield Theatres when he retired on January 5, 1974.

at the Huron Theater in Port Huron. A graduate of Cleary College, he served in the U.S. Army from 1966-67, rejoined Butterfield, and soon became manager of the Palace Theater in Flint, where he remained until moving to the State in 1969. Caryl managed the Michigan at that critical time when it was beginning to fade as a movie palace but was becoming recognized as a historically valuable building, and proved to be extremely helpful with the emerging effort to maintain and promote the theater's valuable Barton organ. He also recognized the theater's potential as a venue for live performance and oversaw the first productions on its underutilized stage in the 1970s, including landmark fundraising galas in 1976 and 1977.[17]

No formal ceremonies marked Hoag's retirement, but a tribute to him by Henry Aldridge was published in *The Ann Arbor News* on Hoag's last day as manager. Lauding Hoag as "the last of a special breed of motion picture manager," Aldridge wrote:

> He knows more about the practical aspects of vaudeville, music, and movies than we would-be scholars could ever learn. This man is a rich storehouse of incredible treasures. Gerald Hoag has made a wonderful contribution to the cultural life of Ann Arbor and I know that he will not be forgotten quickly. Tonight, I will have the great honor of playing the organ during the last intermission at which he will be present. May the shadows of all the many organists, stage show performers, motion picture stars, and the thousands of pleased customers be there to pay tribute to this fine man.[18]

This milestone for Hoag and the Michigan was also marked by an obituary published in *The Ann Arbor News* on Hoag's last day as manager. Hoag's close friend Paul Tompkins, the theater's longtime organist, died on January 4, 1974. Tompkins' legacy, as well as Hoag's, would become apparent as a new era dawned for the Michigan Theater.

NOTES

[1] Gerald H. Hoag Papers, Box 1, Bentley Historical Library, The University of Michigan, Ann Arbor.

[2] The curved-screen version, using three projectors to illuminate the screen and a fourth for the soundtrack, ran at the Cinerama-equipped Wilson Theater in Detroit.

[3] *The Ann Arbor News*, December 13, 1961: "Guthrie seems to have exactly the touch it takes to guide us sophisticated moderns delightedly through the outrageous Victorian never-never land of Gilbert and Sullivan's satire without losing a man of his audience – this in spite of the fact that most of the values G & S were spoofing have long since been spoofed to death."

[4] *The Ann Arbor News* listed the acts for the 1962 show. In true vaudeville tradition there were eight acts: the Rhythm Kings (fresh from a Kay Starr show at Lake Tahoe); the Zouaves "world-famous precision drill team"; comic-impersonator and vocalist Paul Lennon; Jan Wynn, singing star of the WJR *Road Show;* the Ricardeaus acrobatic dance team; master of ceremonies Gus Howard; Russ Weaver and the Michigan Theater Orchestra; and Tompkins.

[5] Most of the plays for that 1962-63 season were staged at Lydia Mendelssohn Theater. Surviving records do not indicate why the Michigan was chosen as the venue for *Virginia Woolf* but it is possible that there was no other theater available during the busy weeks at the end of the semester.

[6] *The Ann Arbor News*, May 1, 1963.

[7] "This note is merely to repeat my verbal thanks to you for all the cooperation received in our production of *Who's Afraid of Virginia Woolf?* at the Michigan Theatre," Schnitzer wrote to Hoag. "I have never had a more pleasant association with any manager and all of us involved – both the U-M Professional Theatre Program and the *Virginia Woolf* management – are most grateful for the helpfulness of your entire staff. I think it should especially be noted that the members of the cast were pleasantly surprised to find their dressing rooms in as good condition as they would in a Broadway house. Every one of them mentioned his appreciation of the accommodations provided for the artists. As for the stage manager, he felt that your staff made his job a good deal easier because of their professional skill and friendliness. Please be sure to give my thanks to all your people. … I hope this is the first of many profitable and successful collaborations for us." Gerald H. Hoag Papers, Box 1, Bentley Historical Library, The University of Michigan, Ann Arbor.

[8] When a 1966 *Detroit Free Press* piece about the new Power Center likened the Michigan Theater's staging of *Woolf* to "trying to watch something in a train tunnel," Gerry Hoag leapt to the defense: "Many great stage shows have played the Michigan, Ethel Barrymore appearing in two of them," he wrote to the

newspaper. "Paul Robeson, Jose Ferrer and Uta Hagen combined to create a memorable engagement of *Othello.* Zasu Pitts in *Ramshackle Inn,* Boris Karloff in *Arsenic and Old Lace.* Kay Francis in *State of the Union* – Helen Hayes in *Victoria Regina* and a host of other stars have played here to acclaim. … I am attaching a few old programs – for no special reason, and closing with the sincere hope that your reference to my beloved theatre was inadvertent and not corrosively intentional." Gerald H. Hoag Papers, Box 1, Bentley Historical Library, The University of Michigan, Ann Arbor.

[9] The name was chosen from Theatre Without a Name contest entries; the first prize was an all-expense paid trip for two to Bermuda. The winning name was "Vth Forum"; it was eventually changed to the less-confusing "Fifth Forum."

[10] *The Ann Arbor News,* December 7, 1966.

[11] Ibid.

[12] *Same Time, Next Year,* starring Alan Alda and Ellen Burstyn, opened on February 16 and ran until April 19, 1979.

[13] "The Battle of the Screens," published in the May 1978 issue of the *Ann Arbor Observer,* detailed these changes in film exhibition and pointed to the end of splitting and the lower operating costs of the mall theaters as the principal causes for the decline of such theaters as the Michigan.

[14] Inspector Vern R. Sicotte wrote: "Your theatre in general looks very good …, and perhaps with some extra discussion with your inside janitors and some help, you can get these items done and once done then they can keep them up. I know you are as interested in keeping this theatre in good order all the time as I am so I know you will do your best to get all items completed, however it cannot be done overnite and I do not expect them to be. Will help you work these out each time I come to town." Gerald H. Hoag Papers, Box 1, Bentley Historical Library, The University of Michigan, Ann Arbor.

[15] Gerald H. Hoag Papers, Box 1, Bentley Historical Library, The University of Michigan, Ann Arbor.

[16] Ibid.

[17] In 1978, Fred Caryl resigned from Butterfield and took a position at the University of Michigan. He was replaced by Barry Miller, who served until August 4, 1979, as the Michigan's third and last Butterfield manager.

[18] Henry Aldridge, "Gerry Hoag Retiring," *The Ann Arbor News,* January 5, 1974.

THE BARTON PIPE ORGAN CONSOLE. MT

CHAPTER 7

THE PIPE ORGAN
IS REBORN

A S THE MICHIGAN THEATER entered its final years as a commercial movie house, a seemingly insignificant event in the spring of 1971 started a movement that would lead to the theater's salvation.

Languishing in the theater's orchestra pit was the Barton pipe organ. It had not been played regularly since 1950, when staff organist Paul Tompkins began performing regularly at Weber's Supper Club and seldom returned to the Michigan.[1] The organ was damaged in the early 1960s when water leaked into the left pipe chamber and soaked wooden pipe chests and electrical switches, rendering at least three ranks of pipes unplayable. Someone, possibly Michigan manager Gerry Hoag, noticed the damage and commissioned local organ builders Gerry Adams and Dick Houghton to make repairs. Organ enthusiast and former Michigan Theater board member David Lau recalled that by the mid-1960s, members of the Motor City Theatre Organ Society had also begun to work on the instrument. A recording Lau made in the theater late one evening in 1968 attests to the fact that some of the Barton was playable at that time.

BEN LEVY. MT

In the fall of 1971, a nucleus of volunteers – David Lau, Ben Levy, Henry Aldridge, John Minick, Howard Rolston, and other members of the organ society – began to meet regularly on Sunday mornings to work on the organ. The group's first job was to remove all pipe work from the chambers – the rooms that contained the pipes – and to clean each one of the more than 1,000 metal and wooden pipes, removing 43 years of dirt and fallen plaster that had clogged the pipes and often interfered with the sound. Once the pipes were out of the chambers, the chamber ceilings were covered with drywall to prevent further damage from falling plaster. Serious wind leaks were also repaired, including a large hole in the metal conduit that ran over the theater's proscenium and carried wind supply to the left pipe chamber. That task was accomplished by tying a rope around Minick's waist and lowering him head first through a small opening in the ceiling above the theater's decorative plaster until he reached the offending hole. Minick's fix, while suspended by that rope, instantly restored proper levels of wind pressure to the organ.

The organ's console also needed repairs. The many small pneumatic devices that powered the combination action (a system that allowed organists to obtain preset combinations of stops at the press of a button) needed to be rebuilt; in addition, many of the electrical contacts were broken and magnets needed to be replaced.

After 10 months of steady work, the restoration volunteers were ready to show off what they had accomplished. On September 30, 1972, a packed house heard the Michigan Theater's pipe organ in an evening concert sponsored by the organ society. The featured organist was virtuoso Lyn Larsen in a performance of solo works and the accompaniment to *The Sheik*, Rudolph Valentino's silent film classic. Larsen's first number, appropriately enough, was *Hail to the Victors*.

Ann Arbor News theater critic Norman Gibson captured the mood and significance of the moment:

It was nostalgia time for 2½ hours last night at the Michigan Theater.

More than 40 years were stripped away as the sonorous Barton organ breathed its first public recital since the early 1930s, when the instrument went the way of theater organists, who went the way of the Great Depression.

Once more, the Barton organ thundered to the pulse of an old silent movie, under the nimble fingers of Lyn Larsen of Hollywood, who at age 27 hardly could be expected to have first-hand recollections of the 1920s. The red and gold Michigan Theatre organ had been silent for 13 years when Larsen was born.

As he did … when the theater opened, Gerald Hoag stood in the lobby of the Michigan, greeting one and all, old and young. Hoag has been a theater manager for well over 50 years and he is well past retirement age, but he continues year after year as manager of the Michigan. …

BEN LEVY AND
ALLEN MILLER. MT

For the past year, buffs of the Motor City Theatre Organ Society
Inc. have been working on the Barton organ in the Michigan. …
Collectively, they spent several thousand hours refurbishing it so it
would be in condition for a public program such as the one presented last night.[2]

The significance of this article should not be underappreciated. It was
the first of several published in *The Ann Arbor News* over the next seven
years that reported on organ concerts, open houses, anniversary celebrations, and other events at the Michigan Theater. This coverage signified
a growing awareness that the Michigan's pipe organ was unique and worthy of preservation. And this awareness of the organ's value soon spread to
the theater itself. In 1972, the Ann Arbor Sesquicentennial Commission
recognized the Michigan Theater as a significant architectural structure in
the community. In 1974, a plaque was attached to the front of the building
in recognition of this fact. (And, in 1980, the theater would be added to
National Register of Historic Places.)

The Lyn Larsen concert was so successful that the Motor City Theatre Organ Society immediately planned a second concert for the following March. Over the next six years, the society sponsored several other events that featured the organ, including silent-film presentations featuring well-known, professional theater organists. Typically, these presentations would begin with about 45 minutes of popular music drawn from familiar shows and films and a sing-along where the audience joined in for enthusiastic renditions of popular tunes. After an intermission, the organist would accompany the screening of the film. Between 1972 and 1978, organists including Dennis James, Gaylord Carter, and Hector Olivera performed in concerts at the Michigan that included screenings of films with such silent-era stars as Charlie Chaplin, Buster Keaton, and Lon Chaney Sr.[3]

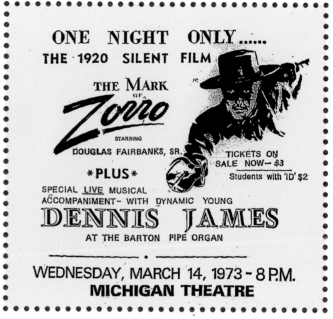

The annual American Theatre Organ Society Convention in July 1974 brought national attention to the Michigan Theater. Held in Detroit, the four-day event included a day trip to Ann Arbor, where more than 500 theater organ enthusiasts from the United States and Canada toured the University of Michigan campus and attended two concerts. A morning concert featured classical organist Searle Wright at Hill Auditorium's famous concert organ; Wright and Helen Dell performed at the Michigan Theater that afternoon. The excellent sound of the Barton pipe organ impressed the audience, which welcomed it as an important addition to the roster of theater organs functioning in their original venues.

Motor City Theatre Organ Society members launched two other important initiatives at the Michigan. The first was a decision that the pipe organ would be played regularly for the public.

At that time, it was the general practice for American Theatre Organ Society chapters to present concerts, hold open houses, and allow private practice time for members once a pipe organ had been restored. Since the Michigan Theater was a fully functioning, first-run motion picture theater when the organ was restored, and because the theater had contributed

several thousand dollars to the restoration effort, the Motor City group made a commitment to have the instrument played regularly. Such a commitment was not easy. It required that the pipe organ receive regular maintenance and that someone be willing to locate organists, establish playing schedules, and act as a liaison when organ events involved the theater staff. Fortunately, volunteer Ben Levy was more than willing to continue as curator of the organ, and until his death in 1998 he devoted countless hours to ensuring the Barton was in top playing condition. In addition, Henry Aldridge agreed to find organists and to establish a monthly performance schedule.

The first organist to play regularly at the Michigan Theater was accomplished pianist and organist Rupert Otto, a social studies teacher at Pioneer High School who also taught music for many years in Ann Arbor. As he brought the restored Barton up on its four-poster lift for his debut on December 23, 1972, Otto played the theme from Gordon Jenkins' *Manhattan Tower;* it would be the signature piece for Otto's overture performances at the Michigan. Many members of the audience were so surprised by the sound of the pipe organ filling the theater as they filed out at the end of the 7 p.m. screening of *The Poseidon Adventure* that they again took their seats to hear Otto's full 15-minute set.

During the next six months, Aldridge and Newton Bates joined Otto at the Michigan Theater organ. Gerry Hoag, thrilled to have the organ as a regular feature, asked that it be played during the break between the 7 and 9 p.m. shows on Fridays and Saturdays. To meet this schedule, Otto, Bates, and Aldridge each had to play three times a month with one weekend off, and they performed on the Barton through the Michigan's remaining years as a commercial theater.

The organ society's other significant initiative was the inauguration of open houses at the theater on the second Sunday of each month to give organ enthusiasts and the public an opportunity to play and hear the Barton. These Second Sundays, which began in December 1973 and continued into the early 1980s, opened with a short recital by a Michigan house organist or a guest artist; an "open console" period that followed gave visitors a chance to play the Barton. The Second Sunday open houses began at 10 a.m. and concluded at noon, before the theater screened the first matinee of the day.[4]

These Second Sundays required planning: Soloists had to be invited, announcements placed in the newspaper, and refreshments readied. Within a few months Barbara and Grant Cook, David and Jo Lau, Robert and Bo Hanley, and Norman and Gena Hornung had emerged as key leaders of the project. Barbara Cook began to publish a monthly newsletter, *Notes From the Michigan,* to provide updates about upcoming events.

These open houses were crucial to the future of the Michigan Theater by

1970S ORGANISTS (L-R)
HENRY ALDRIDGE, RUPERT
WITH ALICE OTTO, BUD
BATES, JIM FORD. MT

drawing a nucleus of individuals who cared about the organ and the theater and who met regularly to hold a public event. This small but tightly knit group came to the theater regularly to practice, repair the organ, or enjoy the open houses, and it developed into an alternate staff that gradually learned how to operate the theater's mechanical systems and discovered the theater's hidden treasures. With regular access to the theater and informed by *Notes From the Michigan*, these devotees were quick to sense how the theater was faring physically and financially. In 1977, the Ann Arbor Sesquicentennial Commission issued a special citation in recognition of the group's efforts to restore the Barton. At a time when social awareness of the need to preserve historic buildings was growing in the United States, the restoration of the Barton pipe organ and its regular public use – along with renewed appreciation of the Michigan's grand lobby, seating capacity, and stage – inspired renewed interest in the theater.

SECOND ANNUAL ST. JOSEPH MERCY HOSPITAL BENEFIT

ST. JOE'S PLAYS THE PALACE

Friday, October 7, 1977 Michigan Theatre, Ann Arbor, Michigan

A fundraiser for St. Joseph Mercy Hospital in October drew more attention to the Michigan and its untapped resources. *St. Joe's Goes to the Movies* brought a host of community leaders to the theater, some of them for the first time. The pipe organ played as formally dressed guests filed in. The red house curtain, not seen for many years, rose at 8 p.m. for a 45-minute vaudeville show, followed by a screening of the 1933 film *Dancing Lady* (starring Clark Gable and Joan Crawford and featuring a young Fred Astaire).[5] A second hospital fundraiser the following year, *St. Joe's Plays the Palace*, ran for three days. The tribute to the great days of the flagship vaudeville theater on New York's Times Square included

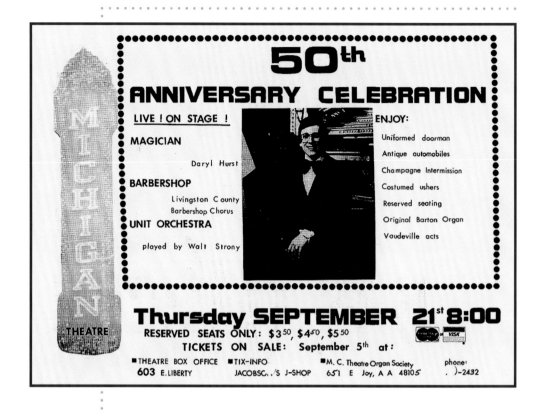

50th ANNIVERSARY CELEBRATION

LIVE ! ON STAGE !

MAGICIAN
Daryl Hurst

BARBERSHOP
Livingston County
Barbershop Chorus

UNIT ORCHESTRA
played by Walt Strony

ENJOY:
Uniformed doorman
Antique automobiles
Champagne Intermission
Costumed ushers
Reserved seating
Original Barton Organ
Vaudeville acts

Thursday SEPTEMBER 21st 8:00
RESERVED SEATS ONLY: $3⁵⁰, $4⁵⁰, $5⁵⁰
TICKETS ON SALE: September 5th at :

■ THEATRE BOX OFFICE   ■ TIX-INFO   ■ M. C. Theatre Organ Society   phone:
603 E. LIBERTY   JACOBSC..'S J-SHOP   651 E Joy, A A 48105   .)-2432

dozens of numbers that recreated routines of such stars as Sophie Tucker, Will Rogers, Judy Garland, and Danny Kaye, and featured the talents of local producers Judy Rumelhart and Irene Connors, among many others. *The Ann Arbor News*, however, lauded the theater itself – "that wonderful old Art Deco house" – as the true star of the show.[6]

The Michigan Theater's 50th year was celebrated in an anniversary show on September 21, 1978. Sponsored by the Motor City Theatre Organ Society, the program featured organist Walt Strony in solo performance and accompanying a silent film and a newsreel from the 1920s. Former managers Gerry Hoag and Fred Caryl and then-manager Barry Miller (appointed in July 1978, he was the Butterfield's last) were present and Master of Ceremonies Henry Aldridge paid special tribute to Hoag, who stood to acknowledge applause from the large audience.

In a piece marking the anniversary for the *Ann Arbor Observer*, Aldridge traced the history of the theater – while suggesting a direction for its future:

The Michigan Theater's 50th year was celebrated in an anniversary show on September 21, 1978.

In an age when many big-city movie theaters of the 1920s have been relegated to showing cheap thrillers and porn, or even demolished, Ann Arbor is extremely fortunate to have a fine example of Hollywood opulence in the Michigan Theater. As the picture palace becomes recognized as the marvelous product of a bygone era, interest in restoring viable remaining examples has burgeoned. Many old theaters have been revitalized by live performances of music, ballet, plays, and lectures that augment film presentations. In Atlanta the mammoth Fox Theater is alive and well. So is the Ohio in Columbus, Shea's in Buffalo, the Tennessee in Knoxville and the Tivoli in Chattanooga. ... As the Michigan Theater turns 50, we wish it a very happy birthday and best wishes for many happy returns.[7]

THE BARTON PIPE
ORGAN CONSOLE.
MT

NOTES

[1] There are no recorded public uses of the organ between May 1950 and 1970.

[2] *The Ann Arbor News,* September 30, 1972.

[3] The full roster of these shows:
September 30, 1972: Lyn Larsen and *The Sheik,* with Rudolph Valentino.
March 14, 1973: Dennis James and *The Mark of Zorro,* with Rudolph Valentino.
October 24, 1973: Gaylord Carter and *The Hunchback of Notre Dame,* with
    Lon Chaney Sr.
April 3, 1974: Lyn Larsen and *Sherlock Jr.,* with Buster Keaton.
November 20, 1974: Karl Cole and *The Rink,* with Charles Chaplin, and *Liberty,*
    with Stan Laurel and Oliver Hardy.
October 1, 1975: Dennis James and *The Monster.*
February 26, 1976: Hector Olivera and a Laurel and Hardy film.
July 22-23, 1976: Rupert Otto and *The General,* with Buster Keaton, and *Phantom
    of the Opera,* with Lon Chaney Sr.
November 18, 1976: Hector Olivera and *The Blacksmith,* with Buster Keaton.
October 13, 1977: Lee Erwin and *My Best Girl,* with Mary Pickford.
April 1, 1978: Gaylord Carter and *Tumbleweeds,* with William S. Hart.

[4] On December 2, 1973, Norman Gibson wrote in *The Ann Arbor News:* "David J.
Lau is one of several Ann Arbor residents who get a kick out of prowling through
the chambers of the Barton organ in the Michigan Theatre. … If you have never
[done this], it's something you might try on any second Sunday of any month….
Anyone who has some experience playing the organ probably will be given the
chance to sit at the console of the mighty golden instrument and play a few bars.
Others probably will be told how an organ works and will get a chance to go
through the chambers, which contain the pipes and other instruments."

[5] Perhaps inspired by the use of the theater's stage for the *St. Joe's Goes to the
Movies* show, Butterfield booked a touring company production of the controversial
musical *Oh, Calcutta* for May 12, 1977. The only other uses of the Michigan Theater
stage in the previous 15 years had been for a pair of productions in March 1976:
a one-night performance of the musical *Godspell* on March 4 and a concert by
Arlo Guthrie on March 25.

[6] The show included Rumelhart (then Judy Manos) singing *Some of These Days,* Irene Connors doing *You Made Me Love You,* and John McCollum performing *I'm Always Chasing Rainbows;* preshow music was played on the Barton organ and the orchestra was led by Brad Bloom. Al Phillips described the event in an article titled "A Glittering Good Time" in *The Ann Arbor News* on October 8, 1977: "Judy Manos and Irene Connor took over the Michigan Theater and for one giddy night, turned the old Metro-Goldwyn-Mayer [-style] neoclassical movie house into something it always wanted to be; that is, something glittering. For one hour before the show began, the producers held a reception and the bubbly flowed. Hundreds of people rolled in in gorgeous costume. … Manos and Connors held a genuine high-style opening with cadets for ushers, so self-confident as to be irresistible. It is a tribute to the theater, that wonderful old Art Deco house, that it dwarfed everyone. You simply cannot be too big for the Michigan Theater."

[7] Henry Aldridge, "The Michigan Theater: A Look Back at the Grand Opening of Ann Arbor's Most Splendid Picture Palace," *Ann Arbor Observer,* January 1978.

THE MODERNIZED MARQUEE. MT

CITIZENS TO

THE RESCUE

AS SUPPORTERS CELEBRATED the Michigan Theater's 50th anniversary in September 1978, some of them already knew that it faced a very uncertain future.

In early 1978, W.S. Butterfield Theatres Inc. informed the Poulos family that it would not seek a long-term renewal of its 50-year lease of the Michigan Theater. The lease was due to expire on December 31 – raising the possibility that at the end of the year the Michigan would cease to operate in its current configuration. In response to Butterfield's announcement, the Poulos family hired Hobbs+Black Architects of Ann Arbor to draw up plans for converting the theater into a retail space.

Quite by accident, the Poulos family's plans were discovered in the spring of 1978 when a Pioneer High School student who worked at Weber's Restaurant in Ann Arbor overheard conversation among Poulos representatives and the architects and saw blueprints spread out on a table. The student reported his discovery to Pioneer civics teacher Rupert Otto, one of the staff organists at the Michigan Theater, knowing that Otto would take a special interest in the news.

By late 1978, Henry Aldridge had brought together a group of local people active in business, the arts, and other aspects of the community who were committed to preserving the community resource.

In July, Otto shared the student's story with Ann Arbor – area members of the Motor City Theatre Organ Society who were gathered for a Sunday picnic at the home of theater organ volunteers Barbara and Grant Cook. Stunned at the prospect of losing the theater and very much concerned about the future of the pipe organ, club members began to discuss what could be done to stop the closure and conversion of the theater. Organist Henry Aldridge took the lead, believing that the Michigan was valuable to Ann Arbor because it housed a performing space not controlled by the University of Michigan. As such, the theater could serve as a community auditorium and attract orchestras, jazz ensembles, rock groups, theater troupes, lecturers, and films that could not find space at the nearby university venues such as Hill Auditorium, the Lydia Mendelssohn Theater, the Power Center for the Performing Arts, and Rackham Auditorium.

Several factors would work in the effort's favor. The theater had an advantageous location near the U-M campus in a healthy retail area surrounded by restaurants, book shops, and clothing stores – directly across the street from Jacobson's, then a profitable department store. The Michigan was also in good repair and attractive despite its modernization in the 1950s. While its dressing rooms, stage rigging, and lighting were dated, the theater could be used as it stood for many types of live productions and film screenings. Aldridge believed the theater could be converted to community use with a relatively small investment.[1]

By the late 1970s Americans had become more interested than ever before in preserving historic buildings. In Ann Arbor, residents in recent years had developed a greater affection for the Michigan and appreciation for its potential because of the pipe organ's restoration and the public events – open houses, silent films, concerts, benefits – that showcased the instrument and the theater's rich past.

Throughout the summer and fall of 1978, Aldridge worked virtually alone in seeking a way to save the Michigan Theater. He enlisted the help of Ann Arbor historian Wystan Stevens, who put him in touch with his sister, Mary Hathaway, and her husband, John, a prominent Ann Arbor attorney. Aldridge also talked with the Poulos family's real estate agent, John Swisher, and with the Michigan's new manager, Barry Miller, who confirmed that there were plans by the Poulos family to convert the theater to other uses.

By late 1978, Aldridge had brought together a group of local people active in business, the arts, and other aspects of the community who were committed to preserving the community resource. The Friends of the Michigan Theater, as the group called itself, included Miller, Stevens, Swisher, Judy Rumelhart, J. Roland Wilson of the University of Michigan Professional Theatre Program, Wilfred Kaplan of the Ann Arbor Council for the Performing Arts, James Packard of the Ann Arbor Summer Theater Festival, Jim Frenza of the Ann Arbor Chamber of Commerce, Thomas Petiet of the Comic Opera Guild, Louisa Pieper of the Ann Arbor Historical Foundation, Emerson Hoyt of the Ann Arbor Symphony Orchestra, *Ann Arbor Observer* editor Mary Hunt, and organ society members Grant Cook and Dave Lau.

The group met in November at John Hathaway's office building at 310 South Ashley Street. There, Swisher described the possibility of converting the Michigan's balcony to a mini-theater and its main auditorium into two or three floors of retail space, while retaining the theater's entrance and grand foyer. He told the group that the assessed value of the theater itself was about $500,000, but that the Pouloses did not really wish to sell the structure. Swisher said he believed that the family felt that it had no choice but to sell in order to guarantee financial security for several family members.

Following the meeting, Aldridge drafted a letter that described the Friends of the Michigan Theater and the organization's goals. He called the "entire Michigan Theater facility … an irreplaceable part of Ann Arbor's cultural heritage" and said the group was "dedicated to the idea that new theatrical uses can and must be found" for it:

Although Ann Arbor already has many fine theatrical facilities, we feel that the use of the Michigan Theater could relieve crowded conditions in these existing facilities, in addition provide a magnet for drawing even more outstanding theatrical events to Ann Arbor. Because of its lovely architectural design, its historical value, and its excellent facilities, the Michigan theater could become an outstanding symbol of Ann Arbor's pride in its past and its interest in the future.[2]

The first public word of the Michigan's possible demise came on December 11 in *The Ann Arbor News*, in an article under the headline "Michigan Theater May Close Doors." Swisher told *The News* that the Poulos family was investigating alternative uses for the space to guarantee steady income and that the theater's interior might be redesigned to accommodate retail use, but added that "plans are pretty preliminary and not definite." Wystan Stevens was quoted as calling the theater's imminent demise "a terrible loss – one for which posterity will never forgive us." *The News* noted that it "marks another casualty of the American theatergoers' changing habits, which forced the closing of New York City's Radio Music Hall and caused the proliferation of clustered mini-theaters throughout the nation."

On January 5, 1979, *The News* reported that the theater would remain open "for the next several months while efforts continue to save the historic structure from becoming a shopping mall or being torn down," and that "a committee called "Friends of the Michigan Theater" has been formed … to see if the theater could be preserved without jeopardizing the welfare of its elderly owners, the family of the late Angelo Poulos."[3]

In spite of the considerable enthusiasm among the Friends of the Michigan Theater, the group had been able to accomplish very little until early February, when Aldridge, John Hathaway, and Ann Arbor Mayor Lou Belcher met at the Old German restaurant and agreed that the first step should be to form a 501(c)(3) nonprofit corporation. With this tax-exempt status, the group would be able to begin meaningful negotiations with the Pouloses. Belcher recommended local attorney Charles Borgsdorf for the job of drawing up articles of incorporation for the nonprofit Michigan Community Theatre Corporation; they were signed on February 9. The founding officers of the MCTC were Belcher, Aldridge, Hathaway, Richard L. Lotz of the Ann Arbor Convention and Visitors' Bureau, and Ann Arbor City Council Member Earl W. Greene.[4]

Within days, the new corporation began negotiations with the Poulos family and W.S. Butterfield Theatres Inc. Two transactions were necessary:

first, the purchase of the Michigan Theater and adjacent office building from the Poulos family, then the acquisition of the theater's furnishings, including the precious Barton pipe organ, from Butterfield.[5]

On Sunday, February 11, *The Ann Arbor News* published "Final Curtain for a Keyboard Paradise," an article with photos of the pipe organ console and the organists who regularly played at the Michigan. Rupert Otto was among the Michigan Theater organists quoted at length describing how much it meant to have the opportunity to perform on the instrument:

> For Otto, who will soon retire from the Ann Arbor Public Schools, the organ is what Ann Arbor is all about.

> "If the organ goes, I don't think I'll have any reason to stay here," he says sadly.

> Otto describes the goodwill that the audience often displays toward the organist as "the best ego builder a person could have."

> His all-time favorite moment occurred when he was playing "My Heart at Thy Sweet Voice" from the opera *Samson and Delilah*. "A beautiful soprano [in the audience] came in on

the chorus," Otto recalls. "Then, in the second chorus, she was joined by a dramatic tenor. The audience went wild."

On the day of the appearance of this article, which conveyed the urgent message that time was running out for this magnificent instrument and that the loss would be tragic for the city, Aldridge invited Mayor Belcher to attend the Motor City Theatre Organ Society's Second Sunday open house at the Michigan. Aldridge took Belcher backstage, showing the mayor that the theater had the potential to present live performances. It was while they were on the stage that Belcher expressed his support for Aldridge's vision of the Michigan as a community auditorium and reiterated his pledge to save the theater from demolition. Belcher's visit was a symbolic turning point in the efforts to save the Michigan, uniting the organ society's enthusiasm and sense of urgency with the resources and expertise of the city of Ann Arbor.

*THE ANN ARBOR NEWS,
FEBRUARY II, 1979.*

The following month, the Michigan booked a special showing of *That's Entertainment* and billed it as "a tribute to the historic Michigan Theater," inviting the public to "re-live for perhaps one last time those wonderful early movie days."

MCTC BUYS MICHIGAN THEATER

On July 31, 1979, representatives of the Poulos family signed an agreement with the Michigan Community Theatre Corporation to sell the Michigan Theater and its office building by land contract for a purchase price of $1.325 million. At the signing, the corporation paid $1,500 – coincidentally, the entire balance of the MCTC's account at the time – and agreed to pay $1,500 a month until the end of 1979. The agreement also required MCTC to make a down payment of 29 percent – $384,250 – by December 31.

At the same time, MCTC signed a $50,000 purchase agreement with Butterfield for various theater fixtures, including a ticket chopper, lamps, microphones, projectors, and the screen. As a condition of the sale, the MCTC agreed not to compete with Butterfield in the commercial screening of films in Ann Arbor; in a separate agreement, Butterfield donated the Barton pipe organ to the nonprofit corporation.

To help pay for the fixtures, Mayor Belcher turned to his friend and supporter of the arts, Margaret D. Towsley. An heir to the Dow Chemical fortune, Towsley had a special fondness for the Michigan Theater; her daughter, Judy, was active in the St. Joseph Mercy Hospital benefit productions and had attended many meetings about the future of the theater. Towsley wrote Belcher a personal check for $10,000 toward the $50,000 purchase – the first of many large contributions she was to make to the Michigan in coming years.

THE POULOS FAMILY WITH JOHN SWISHER AND MAYOR BELCHER. MT

THE MICHIGAN'S FINAL WEEK

Manager Barry Miller scheduled *The Sound of Music* and *Days of Heaven* for the Michigan Theater's last week as a commercial motion picture house; to mark the occasion, organists played the Barton for each of the three daily screenings. *The Sound of Music* ran July 30 through August 1 (Aldridge played his last overture before the 4 p.m. show on Wednesday, August 1). Final organ overture honors went to Newton Bates on Saturday, August 4, before the 9:30 p.m. screening of *Days of Heaven*. After 51 years as a commercial theater, the Michigan closed quietly late that evening.

On the following Monday, August 6, Miller met with Aldridge, who was representing the MCTC. Miller handed over a large ring of keys. "It's all yours now," he told Aldridge, and quickly left the building.

Aldridge stood alone in the lobby for a few minutes, wondering what he had gotten himself into. Then, he turned off the lights and went home.

The next day, the corporation's board of directors – individuals from local businesses, professions, the arts, and the university – took a brief tour of the facility and held its first meeting at the theater (see Appendix B for the roster of founding board members). The 16 members present met the incorporating officers, learned details of the negotiations with the Poulos family, and received a financial report. The new corporation had exactly $2,344.78 in the bank – most of it supplied by the city of Ann Arbor after the City Council voted to allocate $2,000 in startup funds for the new corporation.

On August 21, the MCTC board chose its officers: Richard Lotz was named president; Aldridge, vice president; Bob Johnson, of the local accounting firm Icerman, Johnson and Hoffman, was named treasurer; and local architect Woody Holman, secretary. By this time, MCTC board members had begun to realize the daunting nature of the project.

… Belcher had a plan: The Ann Arbor mayor would ask the city to issue bonds in the amount of $540,000 at an interest rate of 8 percent; the bond issue would finance the purchase of the theater.

Three pressing issues needed to be addressed. The first was the condition of the physical plant. While Swisher Realtors had agreed to oversee the needs of the office-building portion of the property, John Swisher had assumed that the corporation would take care of the theater. On August 18, board member John Briggs, president of International Alliance of Theatrical State Employees (IATSE) Local 395, alerted Lotz to the need for funding beyond rent costs to repair the theater's boilers, pay for an inspection, and cover monthly utility and alarm system expenses.

Briggs took two important actions that would secure the theater's short-term survival: he and members of IATSE would donate their time and talents to the repair of the aging stage rigging, stage floor, and fire suppression system; this would allow live shows to be produced immediately in the nonprofit's early months. Briggs went further: "If there currently exists a problem in having someone available to show the theater to potential users or act as a part-time interim manager," he wrote to Lotz, "I would be willing to make myself available. I have extensive experience in the operation of a movie theater."[6] In the theater's early months under MCTC ownership, Briggs and Aldridge would jointly supervise the management of the theater.

The second immediate issue facing the board was the need to raise money. Little progress had been made on funding issues, and it was clear to the board that it would be unable to pay the monthly rent or the initial payment on the land contract due at the end of the year. At a September 18 meeting, the board decided that unless the city agreed to take over funding of the theater – a monthly obligation of $5,000 – and pay for maintenance as well, the MCTC would close it as of October 1.

The Michigan Theatre Presents

RICK NELSON

TUESDAY, OCTOBER 23
8:00 p.m.

Tickets $8.50 at the door or at these locations:

**WhereHouse Records—Ann Arbor, Ypsilanti
Huckleberry Party Store—Ypsilanti
Falsetta's—Ann Arbor
Aura Sounde—Ann Arbor**

proceeds to support the Michigan Theatre

Fortunately, Belcher had a plan: The Ann Arbor mayor would ask the city to issue bonds in the amount of $540,000 at an interest rate of 8 percent; the bond issue would finance the purchase of the theater. The office building would be split off from the theater and sold. Until the bonds were purchased, the city would pay the monthly rent on the theater. To staff the theater, the mayor's office would provide a pool of workers under the Comprehensive Employment and Training Act (CETA), a federal program that funded training and employment of low-income people. In the first week of November, the City Council backed Belcher's proposed bond issue. In December, the city made a down payment of $162,000 toward the land contract with the understanding that funds would be repaid with revenue from the bond sale.

The third pressing need was to put the Michigan Theater's stage and screen to use so that the new non-profit could claim its place in the city's cultural life.

The third pressing need was to put the Michigan Theater's stage and screen to use so that the new nonprofit could claim its place in the city's cultural life. Volunteers turned their attention to relighting the marquee and scheduling activities in the theater. Board member Karen Young, who was manager of the U-M Office of Major Events, had reported as early as mid-August that several groups had inquired about using the theater. Robin Rennie, a student of Aldridge's at Eastern Michigan University who also worked for Young, volunteered to use the Office of Major Events to book a series of films into the Michigan. Bo Hanley and Barbara Cook led other members of the Motor City Theatre Organ Society in preparing the concession stand for full operation when the theater re-opened.

The Michigan Theater's new life as a community auditorium began modestly, with an organ society Second Sunday concert on September 9. Four days later the Cinema Guild, a U-M film society, screened *The Birth of a Nation* with live organ accompaniment. On Sunday, September 30, the MCTC sponsored its first film: With the showing of *Gigi*, advertisements proclaimed, "Michigan Theater's Screen Glows Again."

Use of the theater picked up dramatically in the remaining months of 1979. October featured seven events, including two film screenings, an Ann Arbor Chamber Orchestra concert, and an appearance by rock star Rick Nelson. November's nine programs included punk rocker and Ann Arbor native Iggy Pop in concert; there were more movies and performances in December, among them the Kiwanis Club's first Christmas sing-along. By the end of the year, the Michigan had hosted 29 events with an estimated attendance of 15,000 – figures that clearly illustrated the need for the theater.

VALENTINE'S DAY SPECIAL
IT WILL TICKLE YOUR FUNNY BONE!
SPENCER TRACY
KATHARINE HEPBURN
Adam's Rib
with JUDY HOLLIDAY
MICHIGAN THEATRE
February 14 Only
Two Shows — 7:00 & 9:15
Come Early To Hear The Barton Pipe Organ

The Michigan continued to be in regular use during the early months of 1980. The highly respected Ann Arbor Film Festival, then in its 17th year, rented the Michigan for an entire week in March.[7] The theater also booked classic films, and most turned a modest profit. The concession stand reported sales of more than $1,500 a month.

On February 26, the Ann Arbor Municipal Finance Commission approved a $540,000 bond issue for the purchase of the theater. Belcher told the commission that one buyer had expressed interest, but six weeks later the bonds still had not been sold. Belcher went to City Council with a revised plan to buy the theater that called for the Poulos family to accept only interest on the land contract's unpaid balance of $378,000 until the bonds could be sold. The city would be reimbursed for those payments from theater-rental revenues. On April 14, Belcher's plan fell one vote short of passage by the City Council.

At that meeting, *The Ann Arbor News* reported, "Belcher turned off his table microphone, looked at council members and said quietly, 'The theater's gone.'"[8] Nevertheless, he was determined to seek another vote from the council, and in the week that followed, Belcher and MCTC board members lobbied council members and drew up presentations for a second City Council meeting, scheduled for April 21. The effort paid off: "Theater Gets Time to Raise Cash," *The News* reported the next day.[9]

Just a few days later, the bonds were sold to Huron Valley National Bank at an interest rate of 6.697 percent; the MCTC's lease with the city obligated it to pay the principal and interest on the bond issue. Said a relieved Robert L. Johnson, who had taken over as board president in January: "Now that we know the size of the task, we can go about the business of accomplishing it."[10]

The board of what was now called the Michigan Theater Foundation now had the task of operating a successful theater.[11] *Meet the Michigan*, a benefit that took shape in the winter of 1980, was aimed at raising money while showcasing to the community the theater's potential. The three-day fundraiser began on Friday, May 2, with "Classic Cinema" – a showing of *Now, Voyager,* the 1942 Warner Brothers film starring Bette Davis and Paul Henreid, and the 1939 Marx Brothers favorite *A Night at the Opera.*

"MEET THE MICHIGAN!"

May 2, 3, 4.

The Michigan Theatre was designed by Maurice Finkel and built in 1928. Over the years this glorious movie house has delighted thousands with each era's artistic fashion . . . from vaudeville and the music of the Big Bands to Hollywood greats. With its majestic lobby, sweeping balcony, and charming pipe organ, the theatre documents the magical world of art and entertainment. We are proud to have, in Ann Arbor, one of the nations last remaining movie palaces.

Between the films, the Barton enjoyed the spotlight with a recital by guest organist Tony O'Brien. Saturday was devoted to a daylong "Community Showcase" of various local arts groups in continuous performance onstage and in the lobby; the "Michigan Theater Gala" that evening featured more music, including a performance by organist Dennis James, and ballroom dancing on the stage after the show. The benefit wrapped up on Sunday with a "Rock 'n' Roll Party" featuring local blues musician Peter "Madcat" Ruth and other acts.[12]

In the minds of the board members and volunteers who had operated the theater since September, *Meet the Michigan* marked the end of a critical phase in their efforts to save the theater. Many of those volunteers were exhausted, and the time had come for a professional manager to take over. Earlier in the year, the board had interviewed three applicants for the manager's job and had chosen Ray Mesler for the post (though it waited until the bond sale went through, in April, to make a formal offer). Mesler, who was 52, had considerable experience in managing nonprofit theaters, including stints at the Embassy Theater in Fort Wayne, Ind., and Florida's Tampa Theater. He reported for work on May 5, 1980, and the newly non-profit Michigan Theater, under the stewardship of the Michigan Theater Foundation, had its first professional manager.

NOTES

[1] A study of the Michigan Theater's stage facilities in early 1979 bore that belief out. Richard Beckerman of the International Alliance of Theatrical Stage Employees Union Local 395 and J. Roland Wilson, executive director of the U-M Professional Theatre Program, estimated that modifications necessary to prepare the stage for live productions would cost about $250,000.

[2] The letter began: "For the past 51 years, the Michigan Theater has been a symbol of the best in film entertainment to generations of Ann Arbor citizens. In addition, its fine stage facilities have made possible the presentation of plays, concerts, and benefit performances. Also, its splendid pipe organ has been used to augment film and theatrical events for several years. The entire Michigan Theater facility has become an irreplaceable part of Ann Arbor's cultural heritage. … The Friends of the Michigan Theater is a group of interested Ann Arbor residents dedicated to the idea that new theatrical uses can and must be found for the Michigan Theater. Following the successful examples of motion picture theater conversions in other cities … we suggest that these uses could include drama, opera, symphonic concerts, jazz performances, ballet, lectures, and conventions."

[3] "Theater Stays Open – For Now," *The Ann Arbor News,* January 5, 1979. W.S. Butterfield Theatres Inc. agreed to extend the lease month to month while efforts to save the theater continued.

[4] The purpose of the MCTC, according to the articles of incorporation, was "to operate a community theater exclusively for educational, charitable, scientific and literary purposes and for the promotion and advancement of the arts including the right … to acquire by sale, lease or otherwise, an historic theater structure, for the purpose of housing the theater." The articles were signed by the corporation's officers on February 9, 1979, and sent to the Michigan Department of Commerce.

[5] The discussions drew attention from *The Ann Arbor News,* which reported on March 16 that Lotz, president of the new MCTC, "was confident Butterfield would continue to show movies at the Michigan Theater until some agreement is reached on its sale, even if that means extending the company's lease for the facility." Lotz told *The News* that the MCTC hoped to make the theater "'home of the Ann Arbor Symphony and the Ann Arbor Civic Theatre' … [and that] other uses could include programs with the proposed summer arts festival."

[6] Briggs wrote: "Apart from the monthly rent, there will be necessities like the boiler repair, an engineer's inspection and utilities expense. There will also be demands for fire and intrusion detection services and action on repair/restoration projects. … A closely related matter is the utilization of the concession stand. At the next meeting I will provide some operating figures from a local movie theater which, I feel, will show the real value of a well stocked and accessible concession stand. (Would you believe a net profit of over 70 percent?) The concession stand

may look tacky, but the potential revenue can't be dismissed. … I have extensive experience in the operation of a movie theater and some experience as an investor/participant in the production of live concerts. I'm also a bonded/registered locksmith and would be available to answer any questions regarding the keying of the theater. In general, I have a personal interest in this project besides representing an interested group."

[7] The University of Michigan's Lorch Hall had been the primary venue for the Ann Arbor Film Festival since the festival's inception.

[8] *The Ann Arbor News*, April 15, 1980.

[9] *The Ann Arbor News*, April 22, 1980: "Almost three hours of intense debate, negotiations and an impassioned plea by the mayor Monday led to an extended lease on life for the endangered Michigan Theater. By reversing its last week's rejection of continued financial commitment, the council agreed to give the Michigan Community Theater Foundation more time to raise money to pay back the city's $162,000 down payment loan, but with some tough stipulations."

[10] "Saved: The Curtain Won't Fall on Michigan Theater." *The Ann Arbor News*, April 24, 1980: Johnson told *The News:* "The foundation has a lease with the city, and that lease is for the amount of principal and interest on the bond issue. … Naturally the lower interest rate means lower payments, and that makes our task somewhat easier."

[11] On December 6, 1979, the board voted to change the name of the Michigan Community Theatre Corporation to the Michigan Theater Foundation Inc.

[12] O'Brien's program included the Toccata from the Symphony for Organ No. 5 by Charles-Marie Widor; Saturday evening's Michigan Theater Gala also featured performances by the New McKinney Cotton Pickers and the vocal group Misbehavin'; Sunday's Rock 'n' Roll Party also included the Steve Newhouse Band, the Nuke-A-Billies, Horatio's Herbal Experience, and Vantage Point.

THE MODERNIZED AUDITORIUM. MT

CHAPTER 9

FROM VOLUNTEER TO PROFESSIONAL ORGANIZATION

THE ARRIVAL OF RAY MESLER in May 1980 was the Michigan Theater Foundation's first significant step on the path to becoming a professional organization. And it became urgently clear during Mesler's tenure that the theater needed professional management. While the theater's quickly filling schedule of film and live shows was evidence of the building's value to Ann Arbor, it also exposed weaknesses in the theater's electrical and mechanical systems and posed a significant burden on what was essentially a volunteer staff.

Mesler brought an academic background in music to the job and had spent his career in performing-arts management. He came strongly recommended by the president of the Embassy Theatre Foundation in Fort Wayne, Ind., where he was director of theater operations. His arrival was greeted with a sigh of relief from a corps of volunteers exhausted by its efforts to establish a functioning board of trustees and figure out how to pay an ever-mounting stack of bills while, at the same time, operating what had become a very busy theater.

The Michigan Theater Foundation initially booked its own films, which for the 1979-80 season consisted mainly of classic movies scheduled with the help of the University of Michigan Office of Major Events. Starting with a screening of *Citizen Kane* in March, the Ann Arbor Film Co-op began to schedule occasional films as well. In August 1980, members of

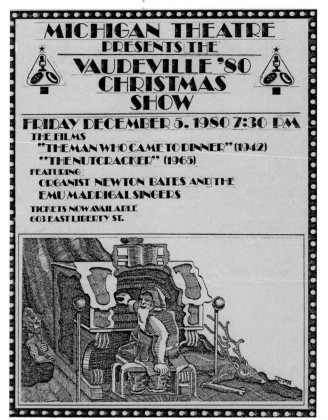

MICHIGAN THEATRE
PRESENTS THE
VAUDEVILLE '80
CHRISTMAS
SHOW
FRIDAY DECEMBER 5, 1980 7:30 PM
THE FILMS
"THE MAN WHO CAME TO DINNER" (1942)
"THE NUTCRACKER" (1965)
FEATURING
ORGANIST NEWTON BATES AND THE
EMU MADRIGAL SINGERS
TICKETS NOW AVAILABLE
603 EAST LIBERTY ST.

the co-op formed the for-profit Classic Film Theater Inc. (CFT) and rented the Michigan for a seven-night-a-week film program. Board members were delighted to find a tenant that would keep the theater open steadily, and by May 1981 had essentially turned over the Michigan's film programming to the CFT. The programming was constrained, however, by the theater's agreement with W.S. Butterfield Theatres Inc. that prohibited the screening of first-run films in direct competition with the State, Campus, and Wayside theaters. CFT instituted a program of classic Hollywood and foreign films, usually on a daily double bill; its first season featured such classics as Hitchcock's *Strangers on a Train*, Francois Truffaut's *Day for Night* and *The 400 Blows, Gone With the Wind, 2001: A Space Odyssey, American Graffiti, Chinatown*, and *Taxi Driver*. The CFT screenings, which would continue until August 1984, attracted a small but steady audience that guaranteed the theater a modest income from the theater's rental and concession sales.

With film programming in the hands of the CFT, the Michigan Theater Foundation devoted more attention to live entertainment and developed two concert series: Vaudeville '80/81 and Concerts Excelsior. Both were ill fated.

Vaudeville '80/81 was pitched as "old-time entertainment, old-time prices at the old Michigan Theater." The series of six Friday-evening seasonal shows included a movie and a mix of live acts featuring volunteer local and regional talent. The first, a Halloween show, presented magician Hank Moorehouse, organist Greg Yassick, and a screening of 1953's *The 5000 Fingers of Dr. T*.[1] Although no specific box office figures for the vaudeville series survive, it can be deduced from other statistics that the shows did not do well. The May 1981 manager's report shows that only 91 people attended the Vaudeville '81 Memorial Day show, and after the first season wrapped with the July 4 program the series was quietly dropped.[2]

Concerts Excelsior was designed to bring a few high-profile ensembles to the Michigan stage, but only one show actually took place: The Irish Rovers performed January 20, 1981, and was a modest success – the theater netted $1,865. While Mesler called it a "glorious experiment," minutes from Michigan Theater Foundation meetings contain no further mention of Concerts Excelsior events.[3]

An electrical-system fire in early December 1980, during an afternoon performance by the University of Michigan Marching Band, was a more frightening sign that pressing issues had been too long neglected.

BURDENED VOLUNTEERS

The Michigan Theater's reincarnation as a nonprofit community resource was a feat attributable to the commitment of its volunteers – particularly members of the Motor City Theatre Organ Society.

In the annals of the rescue of historic theaters, there was substantial precedent for this. The Redford Theatre in Detroit had been saved by a group of theater organ enthusiasts and was being run exclusively by volunteers. A similar model prevailed in Birmingham, where the Alabama Theater was saved by theater-organ lovers; some of them gave up full-time jobs to operate the theater, thus making a transition from volunteers to professional staff.

In Ann Arbor, the dedication of the theater organ group was not matched in size and as the fall 1980 season began there were only a few paid staff positions at the Michigan. In addition to Mesler, janitor Jon Savoie and backstage technical director Jim Haven were paid by the foundation; Classic Film Theater Inc. employed a box office manager and union projectionists. All concession sales and "front of house" duties – box office staff, ticket takers, ushers, changing the marquee – as well as the restoration efforts, were handled by volunteers.

The toll was evident to the board in October, when coordinator Bo Hanley reported that she was having trouble recruiting enough volunteers to staff the concession stand for all the theater's events. Two months later, she resigned in frustration.

GEO. F. KORWIN
COMMERCIAL PHOTOGRAPHE

THE ORIGINAL DIMMER
BOARD. MT

An electrical-system fire in early December 1980, during an afternoon performance by the University of Michigan Marching Band, was a more frightening sign that pressing issues had been too long neglected. The Michigan's original stage lighting system, dating from 1928, consisted of footlights, a few lights hung from an overhead stage grid, and a handful of spotlights recessed into the front of the balcony. All were controlled by the theater's original resistance dimmer board. This minimal lighting system soon proved to be insufficient for contemporary live productions; stage-hands were regularly hanging additional light units and tapping into the antiquated dimmer system for power.

After the marching band concert began, the lights in the theater flickered several times. House manager Henry Aldridge went to the basement to investigate and discovered that the fuse panel was on fire. Mesler called the fire department, interrupted the concert, and quietly directed the audience to evacuate the theater. Firefighters struggled to extinguish the blaze; eventually they dislodged the burning fuses with a wooden pole and doused the flames with sand. This near disaster, along with continuing problems with the theater's ancient heating system, brought home to board members the urgent need to bring the building's electrical and mechanical systems up to code.

For at least a year before the fire, some board members had been expressing concern about the theater's physical condition.[4] In addition to heating and lighting problems, the theater was plagued by leaks, plumbing that didn't work, and a generally shabby appearance. In early 1980, the board formed a repairs and restoration committee headed by local architect Woody Holman, and by spring the panel had established priorities that served as project guidelines for the next few years.[5] From the outset, the intention was to make the theater a safe and modern venue and to restore the building to its original appearance as a movie palace.

In the summer, the committee asked Richard C. Frank of Preservation Urban Design Inc. to estimate construction costs for the rehabilitation of the Michigan Theater. In October, Frank submitted a cost estimate of $5.43 million for the complete restoration of the theater to its original appearance and an overhaul of the theater's mechanical and electrical systems.[6] This estimate was to prove remarkably accurate.

THE ROLE OF THE BOARD

The Michigan Theater Foundation board was composed of two very different groups of individuals. Some had been active at the theater for many years because of their interest in the pipe organ. These board members knew the theater well and had been regularly involved in daily operations. During the theater's first nine months as a nonprofit, many of them had devoted countless hours to cleaning restrooms, mopping floors, changing marquee letters, taking tickets, and running the concession stand. In their view, the Michigan Theater Foundation had a "working" board.

Newer board members were representatives of Ann Arbor's arts and business communities, and viewed the board's role as purely advisory. They

From the very beginning of the Michigan's life as a nonprofit, it was apparent that box office receipts alone would not pay all the operating expenses and finance the restoration; other sources of funds had to be found.

had little actual knowledge of the daily workings of the theater and were largely unaware that a few board members had taken on the lion's share of responsibility for the theater's operations. This split on the view of the proper function of the board inevitably led to tensions, and these made Mesler's job more difficult. Still, during his two years on the job, Mesler and the board kept the theater active, developed an effective board committee structure, outlined a restoration strategy for the building, and established a distinctive community presence for the theater. They were less successful in the critical areas of programming and fundraising.

From the very beginning of the Michigan's life as a nonprofit, it was apparent that box office receipts alone would not pay all the operating expenses and finance the restoration; other sources of funds had to be found. At least three approaches – memberships, seat sales, and a capital campaign with two fundraisers (an auction in August and a "Las Vegas Night"–type benefit for February) – were considered from the outset.

An initial membership campaign was not successful; a mailing of 26,000 brochures between July and October drew only 162 responses. To determine the advisability of a capital campaign, the board that summer also commissioned John Grenzebach & Associates to survey 40 local residents on their opinions about the Michigan Theater and its place in the community. The survey results indicated that it would be a mistake to launch a major fundraising campaign – and also helped explain the failure of the membership drive. The survey found that the community was unaware of how the Michigan Theater operated and lacked a clear concept of the theater's role, and that residents believed that the city "saved" the theater and it didn't need additional funding support – a perception that would hamper

fundraising efforts for at least two more years. Grenzebach suggested that the board concentrate on an aggressive public relations campaign to educate the community about the importance of the Michigan Theater, and that the board form a development council that could concentrate on raising capital. The board agreed to postpone a capital campaign.

Meanwhile, the theater was sinking deeper into the red, falling about $2,000 a month behind in expenses and unable to make the $2,500 monthly lease payment to the city. By December 1980 the theater was $20,000 in debt on top of the $18,000 owed in back rent.

In January 1981 the board formed a development council – and determined that the theater needed to find $70,000 immediately to become solvent. In February, a $10,000 payment on the $50,000 debt to Butterfield was due; board member and Ann Arbor Mayor Lou Belcher again turned to Margaret Towsley, who wrote a check to cover that payment. A "seat sale" launched in March attracted only 13 patrons. That same month, board President Robert L. Johnson made a desperate plea to board members to personally raise $10,000 to $15,000 within two months, but there was no response.

That summer, *The Ann Arbor News* nicely summarized the Michigan's financial situation, pointing out that despite "13,997 paying customers for

87 events in the month of May," the theater was struggling. Mayor Belcher told *The News* that the theater was "having a tough time, particularly on the debt." He continued:

> The city has had to loan the theater some money to make the bond pay-
> ments. At this particular point, we have made the bond payments. I keep
> telling everyone the theater is going to take a couple of years. I still look at
> it very philosophically. We have virtually a civic theater for $525,000 where
> most cities our size are having to spend $5 million or $6 million for a facil-
> ity of that size. It's a great bargain. And we're going to do it. ... The city's
> bought the theater; let's face it. If the foundation doesn't run it, the city still
> owns it. And it's going to succeed, even if we have to pull it through the
> swamps with a rope.

Belcher also discussed the public perception of the theater: "Most citizens read the headlines that say 'theater saved' ... and put it in the backs of
their minds. I don't think it's been brought across that this theater is going
to be restored and thrive based on the efforts of all the citizens."[7]

In May 1981, the board hired A.J. Menlove and Associates, a local fundraising consultant, to develop a plan for a capital campaign. By early 1982,
with debt mounting further, the board directed the consultant to go ahead
with a campaign; Harry and Margaret Towsley were enlisted as honor-
ary chairs and a goal was set to raise $2.1 million by May 1983. In the
meantime, Belcher again stepped forward with a short-term rescue plan,
proposing the City Council put a millage request on the ballot in April 1982
to raise $740,000. Voters approved the millage, financing $200,000 to bring
the building up to code and $540,000 to pay off the interest on the bonds.
The vote forever relieved the theater of its onerous $2,500 monthly lease
payment to the city.

Unfortunately, progress was slow on organizing the capital campaign
– by late summer 1982, some of the fundraising committees still lacked
chairpersons. Donors were reluctant to contribute until the city officially
forgave the theater's debt of $85,000 in back rent; the City Council voted
to do so in October. In November, seeing no evident progress, the board
terminated Menlove's contract. These delays, combined with the stresses of
the mounting debt, caused tensions in the relationship between Mesler and
the board, and by the summer of 1982, it was clear board members had lost
confidence in the manager. In late July, Mesler abruptly resigned.[8]

The board immediately hired Julie Gies as an interim manager and
placed an ad for a new manager in *The Ann Arbor News*.

NOTES

[1] Additional Vaudeville '80/81 shows ran from December 1980 through July 1981, to declining attendance.

[2] Other figures in the same report are also revealing. The theater was in use 28 out of 31 days. Out of 87 events that took place in May 1981, 66 percent were films, 13 percent were live shows and 3 percent were a mix of live performance and film; parties, exhibits, and lectures made up the remainder. Of the 13,997 people who visited the Michigan that month, more than 12,000 came to movies. The bulk of the theater's traffic was due to CFT programming.

[3] *The Ann Arbor News'* January 21 review of the Irish Rovers' performance read: "[T]here was much to celebrate last night; the release of the hostages from Iran and the inauguration of a new president gave the evening a special charge of excitement, and the singing group was in top form to capitalize on it. The performance was a 'glorious experiment' for Michigan Theater producer and manager Ray Mesler, for this was the first time that the Michigan had sponsored a live performance. … 'We sold out of our top priced tickets – 900 of them – two weeks after sales opened. And that's during a recession, mind you,' he says. 'We had people call up for advance tickets that didn't even know where the Michigan Theater is. They are not the patrons that would come to a film club; they are community folks, "townies," and that's just who we want to attract.'"

[4] John Briggs of the IATSE had already written a letter to the board in September 1979, outlining problems with the heating system and making recommendations for repairs.

[5] The committee's first priority was to bring plumbing, heating, and electrical systems up to code. The second was to make necessary repairs to the building and roof. The third priority was to make the stage area more useable by refurbishing dressing rooms, augmenting lighting controls, refinishing the stage floor, obtaining an acoustical shell, and installing a lift for the orchestra pit. The fourth priority was the historical restoration itself: the inner lobby, the outer lobby, and, finally, the auditorium itself.

[6] Frank's estimate included $250,000 for upgrades to mechanical and electrical systems and the installation of a sprinkler system; more than $1.015 million for improvements to the stage area; $1.42 million for interior cosmetic restoration; $375,000 to replace the marquee and restore the vertical sign; and $1.36 million for office and dressing room improvements. The estimate also included a 15 percent contingency of $660,000 and fees of $350,000.

[7] "What's the Future of the Michigan?" *The Ann Arbor News*, July 18, 1981.

[8] "Michigan Theater Chief Quits Suddenly," *The Ann Arbor News*, July 29, 1982: "'That board has got to move quickly and get somebody in there to run that theater,' said Mayor Lou Belcher, a major force behind efforts to save the facility. 'You can't run an operation like that on a volunteer basis. I'm terribly worried about it, to tell you the truth.'"

THE MODERNIZED FAÇADE AND OFFICE BUILDING. MT

CHAPTER 10

NEW LEADERSHIP, NEW FUNDING, AND A NEW LOOK

In November 1982, the Michigan Theater hired a new manager.

Russell B. Collins was a 26-year-old native of Ann Arbor with a master's degree in theater management from the University of Michigan. He had worked with the U-M Professional Theatre Program, the U-M School of Music, and the Black Sheep Repertory Theater, a small company in Manchester, Michigan; in 1979 he founded Arbecoll Theatrics, which presented summer dinner theater at the Michigan League for four seasons. And he was no stranger to the Michigan Theater: Collins produced *Mark Twain Tonight* with Hal Holbrook in November 1981 and *South Pacific,* with the Ann Arbor Chamber Orchestra supplying the music, the following February.

More important than his experience, Collins brought a vision for what the Michigan Theater could become. His knowledge of Ann Arbor gave him a unique perspective on the theater and its relationship to other arts organizations in the community. He recognized that the beautiful building masked by the drab 1956 modernization could re-emerge to take a central role in the arts in Ann Arbor. His role in this revitalization effort would be captured in his statement to the board that opened his interview,[1] in which Collins quoted a report from the Rockefeller Foundation:

A good theater manager is a person who is knowledgeable in the art with which he is concerned, an impresario, labor negotiator, diplomat, educator, publicity and public relations expert, politician, skilled businessman, a social sophisticate, a servant of the community, a tireless leader – becomingly humble before authority – a teacher, a tyrant, and a continuing student of the arts.[2]

In his first four years at the helm, Collins oversaw a number of key developments: new directions in programming, the assembling of a fully professional staff, the Michigan's first successful capital campaign, and progress in building improvements and restoration.

BROADWAY COMES TO THE MICHIGAN

At the same time as the Michigan Theater became available for live music and theater, Ann Arbor's performing arts organizations were making major programming shifts. With the retirement of longtime director Gail Rector, the University Musical Society broadened its scope from the exclusive presentation of classical music to include jazz, international music, and dance under new director Ken Fischer. In 1979, the Ann Arbor Civic Theatre had moved from Mulholland Drive to a new home at the Elks

Club Building at 338 South Main Street. With the appointment of Carl St. Clair as its first paid conductor, the Ann Arbor Symphony became a professional orchestra in 1985. The middle of the decade also saw the debuts of Kerrytown Concert House and the Performance Network, a professional regional theater company.

One of Russ Collins' first initiatives as manager was to broaden live programming at the Michigan Theater. He felt that the existing mix – films booked by Classic Film Theater, lectures, and eclectic concerts – would be strengthened by touring versions of high-quality Broadway musicals and plays. In March 1983, he proposed a season of four shows: a silent film with organ and orchestra, *Amadeus*, Charles Dickens' *A Christmas Carol*, and a return performance of *Mark Twain Tonight*. With the recent demise of U-M's Professional Theatre Program, Collins reasoned that the Michigan was in a position to fill the gap for professional shows. He also believed that it would attract a more sophisticated and affluent audience more likely to contribute to a capital campaign. Collins believed such programming would demonstrate that the Michigan was a first-class venue for live entertainment and as such could make a significant cultural contribution to Ann Arbor. While some members worried that the plan posed significant financial risks, the board approved Collins' proposal providing he could obtain underwriting for the shows. He did.

AMADEUS. MT

Don Juan was the first of several silent film presentations at the Michigan that featured an original score performed by organist Dennis James and the Ann Arbor Chamber Orchestra, led by Carl Daehler.

In October, the Broadway touring show *Amadeus* ran for two nights to sold-out houses – "a success by all accounts," in Collins' estimation. In his report to the theater board, he cited "excellent press coverage" and a more than $10,000 profit, as well as "secondary benefits" of "increased interest in membership, higher community awareness, and proof that the current management can present first-class attractions in our historic community auditorium."[3] In December, the theater sponsored the Omaha Community Playhouse's musical adaptation of *A Christmas Carol,* which, according to *The Ann Arbor News,* featured "a cast of 30, a five-piece instrumental ensemble, elaborate sets and costumes, a sprinkling of favorite seasonal carols and a host of special effects."[4]

Following these successes, the Michigan Theater moved ahead with a new program of touring shows and booked the popular Andrew Lloyd Webber musical *Evita* for April 26-27, 1984. Both performances were sold out, netted the theater a $7,000 profit, and earned a good review on April 27 from *Ann Arbor News* arts critic Christopher Potter, who was especially taken with the cast's freshness and energy:

> *Evita's* road-show entourage … first hit Michigan in March 1982 at Detroit's Masonic Temple. Two years later, the company's back with a virtual instant replay, nary a note or a stage motion out of place – same show, same stars, even most of the singers and dancers look familiar. Yet, in this case, familiarity doesn't breed staleness. It takes a fierce kind of loyalty to sink two years of your life into a single nightly ritual (even if the money's good), and it showed Thursday night at the Michigan Theater. Simply put, *Evita's* cast still sizzles.

Although an unqualified success,[5] the production of *Evita* underscored the need for improvements to the theater building. Collins reported that a few patrons received refunds after they complained of falling plaster dust and a minor plumbing leak, and that more than $1,000 in extra labor and materials was required to prepare the stage for the production. "Until a relatively modest amount of capital improvements are made backstage," Collins told the board, "similar costs will be incurred for each touring show."[6]

In spite of the theater's technical limitations, the board felt sufficiently confident of the success of future Broadway shows that it authorized Collins to book three more touring productions for the fall of 1984: *A Chorus Line, Brighton Beach Memoirs*, and *Sophisticated Ladies*. That season was an artistic but not a financial success. *A Chorus Line* was ultimately canceled and the two remaining shows lost between $7,000 and $9,000 each. Collins suggested that the theater's marketing strategy might have failed to generate the level of interest that *Amadeus* and *Evita* enjoyed, and that the building's condition might also have kept patrons away.[7] In spite of those failures, the Michigan continued to present touring Broadway shows over the next two years: *Torch Song Trilogy* and *Mark Twain Tonight* in 1985 and *42nd Street* and *Noises Off* in 1986. The Michigan would step back from programming these types of shows after the mid-1980s, when the University Musical Society under the leadership of Ken Fischer signaled an interest in booking more contemporary performing arts and theater and presenting them at the Michigan.

NEW DIRECTIONS IN FILM

While the touring Broadway shows had become financially problematic, the presentation of silent films with organ and orchestra would be popular and profitable for the theater. The first "Music and Movie Spectacular," on November 23, 1983, was the screening of Warner Bros. 1926 *Don Juan*, starring John Barrymore and Mary Astor. The evening also featured a performance by the Ann Arbor Chamber Orchestra; Collins produced a live prologue on stage to set the mood. The production spoke to the Michigan Theater's history as a silent movie house, drawing upon the best of the theater's original design.[8]

Don Juan was the first of several silent film presentations at the Michigan that featured an original score performed by organist Dennis James and the Ann Arbor Chamber Orchestra, led by Carl Daehler. Since 1979,

THE PROLOGUE TO
DON JUAN. MT

the orchestra had been performing several concerts a year at the Michigan and had become something of a house orchestra for the theater; conductor Daehler was active on the theater's board.[9] The fruitful collaboration between James and the orchestra developed after Michigan Theater organist Henry Aldridge, who knew James' strengths as an organist for silent films, suggested to Daehler that he use his orchestra in performance with James.[10]

Daehler and James perfected a model for silent film presentation. As part of the 1984 Ann Arbor Summer Festival, the Michigan presented the 1922 version of *Robin Hood*, starring Douglas Fairbanks, again with the original score performed by James and Daehler's orchestra. They united again in October to accompany another Fairbanks vehicle, 1926's *The Black Pirate*.

In the realm of sound film, the Classic Film Theater, which since May 1982 had been booking almost all the films shown at the Michigan, had been failing to collect enough at the box office to cover its rent payments. Some patrons, as well, had complained about the quality of some of the CFT programming. In July 1983, Russ Collins recommended to the board

The passage of the millage in April 1982 had lifted from the Michigan Theater Foundation the burden of a monthly rent payment to the city of Ann Arbor.

that the Michigan take over the booking of films. While this would mean a greater financial risk to the theater (as well as the need to acquire a 16-millimeter projector and hire a few additional part-time staff), Collins argued that the shift would lend a more professional, consistent image to the Michigan's screen offerings and give the theater greater control over its own schedule, allowing it to cancel a film if a better-paying live event became available. Over the next year Collins continued to press the board on the issue, and in August 1984 the board voted to end its contract with CFT and took over the booking of all films. By that point CFT was $13,000 in debt to the Michigan; to partially offset that, the theater kept the CFT's projector. Collins largely continued the CFT's programming emphasis on Hollywood classics and foreign films. But the Michigan's film programming options widened considerably in 1984 when W.S. Butterfield Theatres Inc. went out of business, freeing the Michigan from its agreement with the company that limited the theater's access to new films.[11]

THE FIRST CAPITAL CAMPAIGN

The passage of the millage in April 1982 had lifted from the Michigan Theater Foundation the burden of a monthly rent payment to the city of Ann Arbor. While all operations and capital improvements would be financed by the foundation, the building itself was paid for, and the city allowed the foundation to occupy and operate it for the token payment of one dollar a year. Thus freed, the board turned its attention to a capital campaign and in February 1983, with a new manager in place, named a steering committee to direct the effort. The initial goals were for the campaign to raise $900,000 and for a newly hired professional fundraiser to bring in the remaining $600,000.

As she had done so many times in the past, Margaret Towsley stepped in and gave the capital campaign the push it needed to take off.

Within two months, the committee hired local fundraising consultant John Mecouch to do a feasibility study on a capital campaign. Using questions from a donor survey first used in 1979, Mecouch interviewed board members and community leaders and in September reported that previously held impressions of the Michigan Theater that had been negative or ambiguous had changed for the better: Now, the theater had a positive image in the community. Mecouch recommended the campaign proceed, but suggested that $1 million was a more realistic goal. By yearend, he also advised the board that a successful campaign would require exceptional community leadership and hinted that it might be difficult to launch an ambitious fundraising effort in competition with Ann Arbor's many other arts organizations.

As she had done so many times in the past, Margaret Towsley stepped in and gave the capital campaign the push it needed to take off. Towsley had already quietly made substantial contributions to the Michigan Theater at the request of Mayor Lou Belcher: the $50,000 payment to Butterfield that secured the theater's fixtures and, in December 1979, the then-anonymous gift of $150,000 that covered the original land contract payment to the Poulos family. In December 1983, she made another anonymous pledge, to match up to $500,000 in capital funds raised by the end of 1985. In January 1984, local builder Joe O'Neal was appointed chairman of the capital campaign and Mecouch asked the board of trustees to raise $30,000 among themselves as a demonstration of their commitment to the campaign.

By June 1984 that amount had been raised from the board, another $30,000 had come in from other donors, and Ann Arbor resident Margaret

Cameron, whose family had interests in the Weyerhaeuser fortune, gave the Michigan $100,000 with a pledge to renew the gift at least two times. That total, $160,000, was doubled with Towsley's matching funds.

Despite this substantial support, the pace of fundraising slowed in the second half of 1984. The next year, however, the effort got new leadership with the return to Ann Arbor of Towsley's daughter and son-in-law. Judy Rumelhart and Bob Alexander had for several years been living in New York, where Rumelhart had been active in theater. Towsley encouraged them to take leadership roles in the Michigan's capital campaign and by early 1986, Alexander had become actively involved and the board had named Rumelhart president of the Michigan Theater Foundation. Under their direction, fundraising moved forward quickly and the restoration plan was sufficiently far along that the board could safely borrow $400,000 against capital campaign donations to continue work. Ann Arbor architecture firms Quinn/Evans and Osler/Milling were chosen to plan and design the project, and O'Neal Construction was hired as general contractor.

RESTORATION

From its beginnings, restoring the Michigan Theater to its original 1928 appearance had been a central goal of the Michigan Theater Foundation. Unlike many "rescued" classic movie palaces that merely needed to be cleaned and painted, the Michigan had been significantly altered (by the 1956 modernization) and its restoration would require much more than cosmetic work. Fortunately, the original blueprints were available to inform the project.

Motor City Theatre Organ Society volunteers who had originally rallied to the rescue of the theater believed that these blueprints had not survived. But in the summer of 1979, then-manager Barry Miller phoned volunteer David Lau with a warning: Butterfield officials were on the way to the Michigan to clean out the theater's office, and Lau would be wise to get there first and claim whatever he found interesting. Lau alerted fellow volunteer Henry Aldridge and the two hurried to the theater; there they collected a number of artifacts including mirrors, lamps, and the theater's ornate drinking fountain. While going through a closet in the office, Lau happened to reach around the door frame and there, wedged in a dark corner against the door jamb, was a complete set of blueprints. With that discovery, the theater's restoration became a real possibility.

By January 1986, a general plan had emerged that gave a very visible face to the restoration.

Working with architect Richard Frank of the seminal restoration architecture firm Preservation/UrbanDesign/Inc.,[12] the foundation's facilities and restoration committee in 1981 prepared "A Program Plan for the Restoration of the Michigan Theater" that laid out three restoration phases that fit the foundation's fundraising capabilities. Phase I involved mechanical and electrical work designed to bring the theater into compliance with safety codes; funded by the millage approved in 1982, some significant improvements were made by October 1983. Phase II was the most spectacular portion of the project because it involved dramatic transformations of two public areas – the grand foyer and the auditorium.

From the outset of planning for Phase II, there was some disagreement about where money should be spent. Rumelhart argued that some visible restoration needed to be done in public places so that donors could clearly see how their money would be spent. But some of the work involved less visible, nuts-and-bolts updates that were critical to the operation of the theater. The new Tally Hall construction to the west of the theater had blocked access to the stage loading door and therefore a new one was needed to provide access from the north alley, live productions required better sight-lines on the auditorium floor, and the theater was not properly accessible to disabled patrons. Phase II's mechanical improvements addressed those issues: A new floor would be poured in the auditorium to give a slightly steeper slope and to allow a wheelchair-accessible seating area near exit doors, and there would be repairs to stage lighting, improvements to the cooling and heating systems, and electrical upgrades. And while the higher-profile restoration of the balcony and bathrooms would wait and extensive backstage renovations and an orchestra pit lift were put on hold, much would be accomplished within the $1.05 million budget for Phase II.

OPPOSITE: THE ORIGINAL
WATER FOUNTAIN. CH

"I've finally been able to put together in my mind's eye what the theater is going to look like, and I think people are just going to be dazzled."

—RUSS COLLINS

By January 1986, a general plan had emerged that gave a very visible face to the restoration. The walls of the auditorium would be painted and plaster treatments restored; the seats would be refurbished, new brass rails would be added, and new carpet laid. Historically appropriate light fixtures would be installed, guided by the original construction drawings and a few surviving photographs of the fixtures. In addition, a new central chandelier[13] would provide better illumination for the auditorium – when the theater was built in 1928, ushers customarily used flashlights to show patrons to their seats.

The decorative plaster treatments on the auditorium's side walls and organ grills were demolished in the 1956 modernization. Fortunately, a few pieces of the original plasterwork had survived as rubble in the walls. These fragments were used to make new molds and, along with the original drawings and some photographs, helped the architects to prepare accurate plans for complete restoration, including niches, exit arches, organ chamber arches, and grids.

Paint scrapings showed that the original palette for the Michigan Theater was richly multicolored, with the plaster treatments predominantly red and gold, and had been painted over in the 1930s or 1940s and again in the 1950s. The architects recommended that these original colors be restored, although in a somewhat reduced range to save costs;[14] balcony paintwork was postponed to Phase III, which would also encompass restoration of the façade, ticket office, outer lobby, and balcony and construction of an annex containing restrooms, offices, and a 200-seat theater for film screenings.

The grand foyer was repainted in a fashion similar to the auditorium and new carpeting was ordered to match the original design. The concession stand, located between the two central aisle entrance doors, would be moved to the outer lobby; the vacated area would be restored with wainscoting and the decorative water fountain would be placed in the wainscoting between the doors to Aisles 2 and 3. Beveled mirror panels would be returned to the north and south ends of the mezzanine and historically appropriate wall sconces and chandeliers would be installed.

The theater was set to close on Sunday, May 4, 1986; the work was expected to take several months. A week earlier, Russ Collins discussed his vision for the "new" Michigan Theater with *The Ann Arbor News.* "I've finally been able to put together in my mind's eye what the theater is going to look like," Collins said, "and I think people are just going to be dazzled."[15]

Two major events were scheduled for the final weekend. On Saturday evening, a "Vaudeville Entertainment Spectacular" featured live acts and vintage short films (a free matinee performance was presented for senior citizens), including 1931's *A Broadway Romeo* with Jack Benny and 1932's *Billboard Girl* with Bing Crosby.[16] The theater closed on Sunday with a free screening of *Casablanca*. At the end, Judy Rumelhart took the stage to sing the classic tune from that film *As Time Goes By,* and Aldridge lowered the pipe organ on its elevator to the strains of *Goodnight, Sweetheart.*

On Monday, the construction crews arrived.

NOTES

[1] The board received 50 applications for the post and selected three finalists: Matthew Thornton of Adrian, Michigan; David Siglin, manager of The Ark, a coffeehouse/concert hall that originally served as a community outreach facility for Ann Arbor's First Presbyterian Church; and Collins.

[2] From *The Performing Arts – Problems and Perspectives: Rockefeller Panel Report on the Future of Theatre, Dance, Music in America* (McGraw Hill, 1965, 258 pp.).

[3] The show extended beyond the stage in the presentation of *Amadeus* to include doormen in tuxedoes and pre-performance concerts in a plant-filled foyer. "Patrons were favorably impressed," Collins told the board. "The success of *Amadeus* was primarily due to the fact that Ann Arbor wanted to see this excellent show and they were happy to see it in their community auditorium. Public comment has been very favorable. We have been encouraged to present more touring shows in the future."

[4] *The Ann Arbor News*, December 19, 1983.

[5] In his report to the board, Collins said that three auxiliary concession stands in the lobby and mezzanine for the *Evita* performances increased concession sales by 20 percent over the take for *Amadeus*. A $1-per-ticket service charge (as opposed to $1-per-reservation phone call) brought in an additional $700.

[6] Collins also reported to the board: "The auditorium seats … need substantial work. Many are torn and need to be replaced. … The stage needs a 'cross over' so actors can get from stage left to stage right and vice versa without actually going on stage. The dressing rooms need electrical outlets, new makeup lighting, and improved decoration. There needs to be increased off-stage storage (many of the props were put outside the theater because of insufficient space). The lavatories need new fixtures and electrical outlets. It is strongly suggested that the first substantial capital funds work be accomplished backstage. On the whole, *Evita* proved the Michigan Theater is a good home for touring Broadway shows. With the recommended facility improvements, the Michigan will be a more comfortable and efficient place for Ann Arbor area citizens to enjoy fine music and drama."

[7] Collins also expressed concern about the long-term effects: "The losses we have incurred are very hard to take. It unfortunately is part of the mercurial nature of show business. … [T]he greatest potential loss … is not the short-term financial difficulties these failures create, but the possible effect they may have on the board's willingness to undertake similar projects."

[8] The success of *Don Juan* at the Michigan was also due to the attention drawn to silent film by a recent tour of French director Abel Gance's 1927 *Napoleon*, with

a new score by Carmine Coppola. The film was shown in Detroit and other major U.S. cities, accompanied by organ and orchestra.

[9] The Ann Arbor Chamber Orchestra was gradually eclipsed in the 1980s by the Ann Arbor Symphony Orchestra, which with Carl St. Clair as conductor moved to the Michigan Theater for its 1985/86 season (since then, the A2SO has made its home there). The chamber orchestra canceled its April 1986 concert at the Michigan following a dispute between the theater's board and orchestra members over whether, for tax purposes, the musicians should be treated as independent contractors or theater employees.

[10] Daehler first worked with James in 1982 when he conducted the Columbus Symphony Orchestra at the Ohio Theater in Columbus for a screening of the 1922 *Robin Hood.* By 1984, the pair had adapted scores for four films, and had also performed their silent-film repertoire with the Chicago Lyric Opera and the Seattle Symphony Orchestra.

[11] Michigan's film program for October 1984, for example, included *Raging Bull, Popeye, It Happens Every Spring, Modern Times, Willy Wonka and the Chocolate Factory, Alice's Restaurant,* and *42nd Street.*

[12] In addition to pioneering many preservation ideas, Frank trained a group of young architects who shared his vision. Among these were Michael Quinn, David Evans, and Eugene Hopkins. All three, through their own firms, would work on the theater's restoration.

[13] The chandelier was originally intended for the balcony, but the balcony restoration was eliminated from the plan and not accomplished for several years. It was designed by Quinn Evans based on a chandelier in Orchestra Hall in Detroit.

[14] Conrad Schmitt Studios Inc. of New Berlin, Wisconsin, was hired for the painting and plaster restoration of the auditorium and grand foyer.

[15] "The Michigan's New Clothes," *The Ann Arbor News,* May 2, 1986.

[16] The "Vaudeville Entertainment Spectacular," sponsored by the Michigan Consolidated Gas Retirees Club, also featured Bud Bates on the Barton organ, the Galliard Brass Ensemble performing ragtime favorites, and popular songs sung by local singers John McCollum and Julia Broxholm.

THE RESTORED GRAND FOYER. CH

CHAPTER 11

A Restored
Theater, A Revised
Strategy

With some scaffolding still standing, the Michigan Theater reopened to audiences on Saturday, September 20, 1986, with a screening of *Singin' In the Rain.* "The show did go on," *The Ann Arbor News* reported the next day. "Word came at 3 p.m. Saturday, just one hour before the Michigan Theater was set to open its doors for the first time in four months. The newly renovated theater had passed the white-glove treatment by Ann Arbor Building Department electrical inspectors." [1]

The work had begun in the auditorium in May, with crews sealing off the organ chambers and building a protective covering over the organ console. The seats were removed from the main floor and sent away for refurbishing while a new sloping floor was poured; provisions were made for installing additional stage lighting. Scaffolding went up and the auditorium was repainted, the walls containing the organ grills were rebuilt, and on the side walls, niches, and faux exits were reconstructed. When patrons returned that September, they beheld the original gold, blues, and reds restored to the grand foyer, and a plush reproduction of the original 1928 carpet was beneath their feet. Beveled glass mirrors shone from the mezzanines. As they entered the auditorium, they saw a sparkling, multi-colored proscenium and ornate wall treatments, all illuminated by period wall sconces, glittering lights from fixtures hung under the balcony, and the custom-made central chandelier suspended from the auditorium ceiling.

AUDITORIUM SCAFFOLDING
DURING RESTORATION. MT

By October the theater was fully functioning, with a schedule of feature films and a fall lineup of live shows that included magician David Copperfield, composer and performer Philip Glass, comedian David Brenner, and the Chicago-based improvisational comedy troupe Second City.

The formal rededication waited until the last weekend of January 1987, when foundation president Judy Rumelhart's newly formed Peninsula Productions presented three performances of Leonard Bernstein's *Mass*, a challenging work demanding the use of many different musical and theatrical ensembles. *Mass* at the new Michigan involved a number of local arts groups, including the Ann Arbor Symphony Orchestra, the Ann Arbor Cantata Singers, the J. Parker Copley Dance Company, Ann Arbor Civic Theater and an ensemble formed specifically for *Mass* that would become the Ann Arbor Boy Choir. [2]

Opening night of *Mass* on January 29 won raves. *The Ann Arbor News'* Susan Ludmer-Gliebe wrote:

> The re-dedication Thursday night of the opulent Michigan Theater, that Byzantine-Baroque-Gingerbread-Moorish-Romanesque-Classical (all circa 1928, of course) gilt and gold 1,720-seat picture palace, that orna-

THE MICHIGAN THEATER

mental treasure of rococo, with its bronze fountain one expects is gurgling to the muses themselves, with its gloriously hand-painted ceilings harking to the heavens above – isn't that an event any sybaritic Roman worth his or her grapes would attend? … This was a celebration of almost a decade of first saving and then restoring the municipally owned Michigan, and it was worth waiting for.[3]

News music critic Jim Leonard applauded the production:

Bernstein's gaudy, garish, and glorious vision of the crisis of faith was given a performance at the Michigan Theater Thursday night which would have made the grand ol' man of American music smile with pride. … Ultimately, it's the people of Ann Arbor who should be proud that their town has, at last, its own community auditorium; or, in the words of Mayor Edward Pierce, an American equivalent of a European town's "fancy opera house."[4]

NEW AMBITIONS

The re-dedication marked the beginning of an ambitious new direction for the Michigan Theater. The goal was to change the public's perception of the building as simply a movie house and to create a new profile as a center for live performing arts in Ann Arbor that drew the same sophisticated audiences that supported the University Musical Society.

Toward that end, the Michigan board in 1987 identified two sets of live programming it would present: traditional theatrical plays including productions by established national companies, under a Drama Season label; and a range of more experimental performance art through what was dubbed the Serious Fun! Series.

Serious Fun was launched in the 1987/88 season, and it was ambitious. It included the Kronos Quartet; Sankai Juku; *Koyaanisqatsi-Live,* which featured a Philip Glass ensemble performing the score; *Two Can Play* by the Negro Ensemble Theater; Meredith Monk's *Book of Days: A Music Concert With Film; Kabuki Macbeth;* and a Peninsula production of *Peter Pan.* The "blend of avant garde and multimedia events," Collins told the board in a yearend summary of the theater's operations, was "highly successful both at the box office and critically." Serious Fun, he wrote, "created a programming niche for the theater by identifying a target audience of the 'under-40 crowd' which attends the avant garde events, but has little product to choose from."

Collins also reported that outside organizations were continuing to use the theater. More than 16 nonprofit groups – the Ann Arbor Symphony Orchestra, Ars Musica, Comic Opera Guild, and Ann Arbor Civic Theatre among them – had booked presentations at the theater during the 1987/88 season. Other promoters offered a range of rock, folk, and reggae performances; there were special presentations for children and families;[5] even business groups were using the theater, for meetings.

PRISM PRODUCTIONS

The theater was also becoming known as an excellent venue for jazz, folk, and rock. Prism Productions was particularly instrumental in bringing high-profile contemporary music to the Michigan. Prism was formed in 1979 by Tom Stachler of Fowlerville, Michigan, who had been in auto sales before getting into the entertainment industry. He was soon joined by Lee Berry, who had worked for Eclipse Jazz, a booking organization that was part of the University of Michigan Activities Center. Together they brought a new British band, The Police, to the Michigan for a landmark November 1979 concert, just weeks after the theater had been reopened as a non-profit. Board members at the time were leery of hosting such a potentially rowdy event, but the concert's success won them over and rock concerts became a mainstay of live productions at the Michigan.

In the early 1980s, Prism brought in such performers as The Cure,

Laurie Anderson, Simple Minds, and The Replacements. An appearance by blues legend B.B. King in April 1987 was sold out; over the next two years such artists as the Red Hot Chili Peppers, John Lee Hooker, k.d. lang, and Bob Dylan would perform at the Michigan. Prism was also instrumental in bringing the Ann Arbor Blues and Jazz Festival to the theater in the early 1990s.[6]

Prism Productions made two important contributions to Michigan Theater. First, the booker's programming was lucrative for the theater, which received not only a flat rental fee but also a percentage of the box office. The totals, which ranged from $5,000 to $10,000 per event, represented a sizeable amount of revenue. And a more lasting benefit was its role in expanding the theater's demographic in terms of patronage and potential donorship. The groups booked by Prism attracted a young and enthusiastic audience to the Michigan and one different from those who attended films and concerts of classical music. To this younger group, the Michigan became known primarily as a venue for popular music, and as years went by, this audience would mature, prosper, and return to the Michigan Theater as a new donor base.

DETAIL IN RESTORED GRAND
FOYER. CH

Silent films presented with orchestra and organ accompaniment continued to draw audiences. In June 1987, the 1921 Douglas Fairbanks swashbuckler *The Three Musketeers* was screened with the Ann Arbor Chamber Orchestra and organist Dennis James performing the original score by Louis F. Gottschalk. The 1926 film *La Boheme,* starring Lillian Gish and John Gilbert, was presented in February 1988 as part of the Serious Fun! Series.

In 1991, Michigan Theater engaged conductor and renowned musicologist Gillian Anderson, who specialized in using original scores preserved at the Library of Congress to reconstruct performances accompanying silent films. Using the organ and a 25-piece orchestra, Anderson's first offering was *Intolerance,* D.W. Griffith's 1916 epic, in November; a screening and performance of 1924's *The Thief of Bagdad,* starring Douglas Fairbanks, followed in September 1992. Soon Anderson's appearances were a semi-annual affair at the Michigan, contributing to the theater's growing international recognition as a quality venue for silent film.[7]

FINANCIAL PROBLEMS

Based upon the overall success of the 1987/88 Serious Fun! Series, the theater board approved another ambitious schedule for 1988/89. By March 1989, however, the financial picture was not good. While many of the live productions had been critical and artistic successes, they had failed to make money. In May, foundation treasurer Bruce Shapiro reported a budget deficit of $70,000. Though film programming was also performing below expectations, Collins acknowledged that the shortfall could be traced largely to live programming – Serious Fun had been expected to net $8,000 for 1988/89, but lost nearly $30,000. The theater borrowed $25,000 to cover immediate losses and trimmed the Serious Fun, Drama, and Not Just For Kids programming for the 1989/90 season.

Still, the season's artistic quality was notable. Among the offerings were *1000 Airplanes on the Roof*, with music by Philip Glass and script by *M. Butterfly* playwright David Henry Wang; jazz from the Art Ensemble of Chicago; the Kronos Quartet with the Electric Phoenix vocal quartet; and the Flying Karamazov Brothers. The Michigan Theater's Drama Season debuted in 1989 with Hal Holbrook in *Mark Twain Tonight,* a one-man show with Christopher Plummer, Colleen Dewhurst in *My Gene*, the Alley Theater's production of Arthur Miller's *A View From the Bridge,* and Neil Simon's *Broadway Bound.*

Commenting on the Drama Season, Christopher Potter of *The Ann Arbor News* wrote that "a quick glance … is enough to leave you wondering how much more versatile a playbill could get. Spanning Noel Coward to South African guerrilla theater to Christopher Plummer to P.D.Q. Bach, it's a season that seems creatively geared to the principle of something for everyone."[8]

But the losses continued, totaling $60,000 for 1989.[9] As the Michigan Theater Foundation marked its 10th anniversary, Russ Collins told the board that while the Michigan remained the most cost-efficient organization of its kind in an arts community where it had firmly established its place, the financial loss would force the theater to reexamine its priorities.[10]

Collins spent the winter of 1991 in Washington, D.C., participating in an arts management fellowship program at the National Endowment for the Arts.[11] The following summer, he studied the operations of the Michigan Theater as an "inside consultant" and identified key issues to address in a revised strategic plan. Collins argued that the Michigan was "a 'second tier'

There were a number of factors contributing to the theater's budget shortfall: Ticket sales suffered during the 1991 Gulf War, the state sharply cut funding from the Michigan Council for the Arts, and the economy declined in general.

organization ... considered secondary to people's primary cultural interest." Primary interests, he maintained, included such organizations as University Musical Society, Ann Arbor Civic Theatre, and the Ann Arbor Symphony Orchestra. The Michigan, Collins wrote, "is Ann Arbor's 'Arts Utility' – people don't think much about the fact that the theater is here every day but would desperately miss it if it was gone."[12]

Collins also observed that too much of the theater's revenue came from "highly variable sources" – live shows and films, corporate sponsorship of those programs, and concessions. And most of those resources were in turn allocated to programming, leaving support for care of the facility itself in short supply. Collins would conclude that the theater's diverse programming had blurred its marketing image in the community. Was the Michigan a home for traditional drama, experimental theater, pop and rock music, or movies? Perhaps it was time to define a more specific purpose. Collins also noted that 85 percent of the theater's income came from ticket sales; the average was 55 percent for similar performing arts organizations. Clearly, the Michigan needed to develop new fundraising strategies.

That need was especially important as projections for fiscal year 1991 pointed to a $95,000 loss. There were a number of factors contributing to the theater's budget shortfall: Ticket sales suffered during the 1991 Gulf War, the state sharply cut funding from the Michigan Council for the Arts, and the economy declined in general. But specific to the theater itself, fundraising fell short of growth targets and live programming continued to lose money. The board expressed doubts that live presentations could continue in the face of inadequate audience support.

THE RESTORED AUDITORIUM
WITH SCREEN. CH

A NEW EMPHASIS ON FILM

For the remainder of the 1980s the Michigan continued to run classic films and second-run hits, and began to add first-run art house titles for which its only competition was the Ann Arbor Theaters, which had replaced the old Fifth Forum and split into a two-screen facility. With the exception of Cinema Guild, the University of Michigan film societies had ceased operations during the same period as the declining cost of video cassette players and the increasing number of classic and contemporary films available on video pulled audiences from repertory film theaters nationwide.

When it went out of business in 1984, W.S. Butterfield Theatres Inc. sold its remaining Ann Arbor theaters – the State, the Wayside, and the Campus – to the Midwestern Kerasotes Theatres chain. The company was

THE RESTORED ORGAN
GRILLES. CH

notorious for neglecting the condition of its theaters, and soon all three local houses were plagued by poor projection, bad sound, and deteriorating
interiors. In the space of a few months in 1987, Kerasotes abruptly closed
the Campus Theater, long a home for foreign films, and sold the State Theater (which Butterfield in 1979 had converted to four smaller theaters) to
Tom Borders, who converted its main floor to retailing space. The Wayside,
a once-huge single-screen theater that was twinned by Kerasotes in 1984,
closed in 1989. That left the Michigan as the only single-screen traditional
movie theater in downtown Ann Arbor.[13]

The Michigan responded in part by expanding its projection capability.
In 1989, to show a newly available print of the classic film *Lawrence of
Arabia,* the theater purchased a 70-millimeter projector and enhanced
sound system.[14] This addition gave the Michigan an extremely versatile
film projection system that enabled it to screen 16-, 35-, and 70-millime-
ter films; variable speed motors on the 16- and 35-millimeter projectors
allowed the theater to show silent films at their proper speeds of 18 to 24
frames per second.

IRVING SMOKLER AND MIRAMAX

A turning point in the theater's new emphasis on film was the March 1992 appointment of Dr. Irving A. Smokler, a psychologist at University of Michigan Hospitals, as chairman of the board's film committee. Smokler, a passionate film enthusiast who as a student had been active with the U-M Cinema Guild, was the son of a successful real estate developer and head of the Smokler family's KMD Foundation. Over the next several years, Smokler took a lead role in refashioning the Michigan's image as a home for new independent and foreign films as well as classic movies and silents presented with care and authenticity. He helped develop new relationships with distributors, brought new films to the theater, and helped the organization recognize the need for additional screens.

As the Michigan Theater moved to the forefront as a venue for first-run films, that need for additional screens was made even more apparent by the competition for space with other uses for the theater. By 1991, Prism had taken the lead as the exclusive concert promoter for the Michigan and used the theater as its principal venue. A host of other organizations continued to use the stage as well, from the Ann Arbor Symphony Orchestra and the Comic Opera Guild to lectures and fundraisers and parties and weddings, thus making the auditorium less available for the screening of films.

In the late 1980s the Michigan Theater developed a relationship with Miramax, a New York-based independent film company founded in 1979 by Bob and Harvey Weinstein. Miramax introduced a number of outstanding art-house motion pictures to American audiences in the 1980s and '90s, helping to bring about a renaissance in independent film with such releases as *Sex, Lies, and Videotape; Tie Me Up! Tie Me Down!; Pulp Fiction;* and *The Crying Game.*[15]

The Michigan's need for additional screens was vividly apparent with the success of *The Crying Game.* The film opened in January 1993 and played for almost six weeks to large crowds. But the second weekend of its run, screenings had to be canceled because of a previously contracted concert by the Ann Arbor Symphony Orchestra. And the problem came to a head in December with the screening of *The Piano,* another Miramax-distributed film that did very well at the box office but was moved to the State Theater to make room for a previously booked live production of *A Christmas Carol.*

Miramax was displeased, and the Michigan Theater had a problem.

NOTES

[1] *The Ann Arbor News*, September 21, 1986: "'We were going full speed like we were going to open because we had no choice, but we were keeping our fingers crossed,' said theater promotions coordinator Carla Baden. 'The electricians worked overtime all week.'"

[2] On January 3, 1987, Christopher Potter of *The Ann Arbor News* wrote: "Wouldn't it be neat if Ann Arbor's diverse artistic groups joined forces occasionally in one gigantic multimedia entertainment bash? That's the utopian dream spurring A2's newly formed Peninsula Productions, whose founding impresarios say they're committed to the principle of friendly collaboration in cultural endeavors. In fact, it's already more than a dream: come January 29-31, Peninsula will sponsor the Ann Arbor premiere of Leonard Bernstein's *Mass*. ... The purpose of the company is simply to try to put together an organization that can merge Ann Arbor's diverse talents together now and then."

[3] *The Ann Arbor News*, January 30, 1987.

[4] Ibid.

[5] In an important development, the Program Committee in 1989 proposed a schedule of live shows specifically for families and children. It began with the 1990/91 season and eventually became known as the Not Just for Kids Series.

[6] In 1987, Lee Berry bought Prism Productions from Stachler and, in 1999, sold it to an organization that eventually spun it off as the concert promotion company Live Nation. In 2004, Berry joined the Michigan Theater as marketing director.

[7] Throughout the 1990s, silent films continued as a popular offering at the Michigan Theater. In addition to Anderson's appearances, there were the annual Halloween screenings of *Nosferatu* with organ accompaniment. In 1995/96, the theater created an ambitious Sound of Silents Series that featured six films, including *Greed*, with an original piano score by University of Michigan composer William Bolcolm; *The Merry Widow*, with piano accompaniment created by Art Stephan of the Ann Arbor Silent Film Society; *Ben Hur*, accompanied by Anderson's orchestra; and *Metropolis*, with organist John Lauter.

[8] *The Ann Arbor News*, September 10, 1989.

[9] The Serious Fun box office continued to disappoint in 1990/91. In return engagements, the Flying Karamazov Brothers sold only 800 tickets compared to 1,400 two years earlier. *Koyaanisqatsi – Live* sold out only one house compared to two in 1988. Programs for children did well that season.

[10] Collins told the 1990 annual meeting of Michigan Theater members that more than 130,000 people had attended events at the theater in 1989 and that 80 percent of the Michigan's revenue had come from ticket sales.

[11] Deborah Polich-Swain served as interim managing director of the theater in Collins' absence.

[12] *1991 Strategic Planning Process,* report to Michigan Theater Board of Trustees, distributed May 22, 1991.

[13] In 1988 new competition emerged on the edge of town when National Amusements opened the 14-screen Showcase theater complex on the site of the old Ypsi/Ann Drive-In, near the intersection of US-23 and Interstate 94.

[14] The projector purchase owed much to a $45,000 gift from the Herrick Foundation.

[15] The Michigan would ride this wave, screening *Strictly Ballroom, Like Water for Chocolate, El Mariachi, Tous les Matins du Monde, Wide Sargasso Sea, Indochine, Un Coeur un Hiver, The Wedding Banquet,* and others.

THE SCREENING ROOM INTERIOR. MT

CHAPTER 12

PHASE III: RESTORING THE OLD, CREATING THE NEW

When Miramax stopped providing films to the Michigan Theater[1] after a live show bumped *The Piano* to the second-tier State Theater in January 1993, Michigan's scheduling problems came into sharp focus. Without access to Miramax product, the film program would be in jeopardy. Without easy access to additional screens, the Michigan would almost certainly continue to run afoul of film distributors.

To help with future film bookings and to improve relationships with distributors, the theater hired California-based booking agent Jan Klingelhofer, who focused on advising independent theaters, to schedule its films.[2] This move also freed Russ Collins from film-booking duty, which he had shouldered for nine years since the demise of Classic Film Theater in 1984. Collins was able to turn his full attention to bigger issues: where to locate additional Michigan Theater screens, how to complete the restoration of the historic theater – a central goal of the founding board members – and how to pay for those separate but closely related projects.

Since the Michigan became a not-for-profit community organization in 1979, it had depended heavily upon the generosity of Margaret Towsley. On a number of occasions she had written personal checks for as much as $50,000 to fund specific projects or to cover yearly operating deficits. She had also given $500,000 to the Michigan Theater's first capital campaign, led by Judy Rumelhart, her daughter. Even before Towsley's death in 1994, it was clear that the theater would have to find a fundraising structure that would both sustain annual operations and finance the remaining work on restoration of the historic theater.

AMBASSADOR RON WEISER.

MT

In March 1993, the Michigan Theater Foundation board created a development committee to raise money for several projects to update and restore the theater. But in December 1994, in a new approach designed to encourage the participation of potential philanthropists and others with influential connections to the community in the Michigan effort, the existing board was split into separate fundraising and administrative arms. The development committee was renamed the board of trustees and Ron Weiser, owner of McKinley Properties and an influential civic leader, became its chairman; as such, he would lead the theater's new capital campaign.[3] The old Michigan Theater Foundation board became the board of directors and was charged with overseeing theater operations; film committee chairman Irving Smokler was named its president in February 1995.

SMOKLER'S GIFT

The first major gifts of the capital campaign were central to achieving the objective of additional screens – and were essentially an inside affair. Because the theater was bounded by properties on two sides and Liberty Street on another, the backyards of two houses on Washington Street and the rear portion of the Cadillac Building were the only possible locations for an annex.[4] Envisioning their use in theater expansion plans, Smokler in 1994 quietly purchased the properties with his own funds.

With the Washington Street properties secured, Collins, Weiser, Smokler, and Michigan Theater facilities manager J. Scott Clarke began laying plans in early 1995 to complete the restoration of the historic theater and build the new annex. These twin objectives were immediately and enthusiastically approved by the governing boards and in February 1995 Weiser asked his associate at McKinley Properties, chief executive officer Albert Berriz, to survey the theater and provide an estimate of how much the remaining restoration work would cost. Berriz recommended the theater raise $3.5 million, but this amount increased to more than $6.5 million as construction and restoration costs escalated. The restoration would eventually include updating the theater's heating, ventilation, and

The plan for the screening room annex saw a number of revisions before taking final shape in September 1997.

air conditioning systems; the renovation and expansion of restrooms; the restoration of the outer lobby, the Liberty Street façade, and the balcony; and improvements to the backstage area.

Weiser told *The Ann Arbor News* that those goals, along with additional screening space, were essential to preserving the Michigan Theater for future generations:

> If we don't do these things, the theater will slowly deteriorate. Twenty years from now, this will no longer be a jewel of Ann Arbor. I want my great-grandchildren to be able to enjoy this theater. We want it around 100 years from now.[5]

Over the next 24 months, the capital campaign made significant progress. Smokler pledged to fund a portion of the construction costs for the annex, and the theater's two boards approved a five-year, 50-cent surcharge on all admission prices to raise $750,000. In August 1996, the Towsley Foundation awarded the theater a five-year grant of $500,000.[6] In May 1997, the board of trustees reported that the capital campaign had collected $2.2 million in pledges and grants; also that month, the theater received a $250,000 Cultural Facilities Grant from the state of Michigan. By March 1998, a $400,000 challenge grant from the Kresge Foundation would raise the total of gifts and pledges to the capital campaign to $3.4 million.[7]

THE ANNEX TAKES SHAPE

The plan for the screening room annex saw a number of revisions before taking final shape in September 1997. The final drawings showed a new 200-seat theater built in the backyards of the Washington Street properties and new restroom facilities and staff offices placed in the rear portion of the Cadillac Building. The annex would be reached through a door at the north end of the lobby of the historic theater that opened onto a corridor leading to the new theater and restrooms.

Construction faced unexpected delays. The site itself was difficult to reach because it was hemmed in by existing structures. Eventually, access was obtained via a driveway located behind University of Michigan's Lane Hall, located on the corner of Washington and State streets. By the summer of 1997, the site had been cleared for construction of the new screening facility, and the rear portion of the Cadillac Building was reconfigured for

the new restrooms and offices. By September, the shell of the new theater was in place.

Another challenge was designing the interiors of the new space so that they suggested a connection to the historic theater without the expense of copying its ornate details.[8]

To achieve this, certain features, such as the wainscoting and pattern of the carpeting, would be carried over from the historic theater. Dark wainscoting covered the bottom third of the Screening Room's side walls and blue fabric draped the padded the middle section. The crowning glory of the Screening Room's décor was a colorized mural designed by Collins that depicted Ann Arbor's bygone movie theaters. Images of the Whitney, Orpheum, Wuerth, Majestic, Arcade, and Star, as well as other local performing arts landmarks such as Hill Auditorium and Burton Tower, were enlarged and colorized from historic photographs, placed on Styrofoam backing, and attached to the upper side walls.

THE SCREENING ROOM
PROSCENIUM. CH

THE SCREENING ROOM
SEATS. CH

The 200 seats for the new theater, now officially called the Screening Room, suggested a 1920s design with wooden frames and deep red fabric. They were installed in staggered rows so that no seat was directly behind another – a detail that meant clearer sight lines for the audience – and faced a 20-foot-by-29-foot screen that also had been positioned for an unobstructed view.

The Michigan Theater Screening Room opened on October 1, 1999, with a showing of the 1998 film *Illuminata,* whose score was written by U-M music professor William Bolcolm. Christopher Potter of *The Ann Arbor News* lauded the "both elegant and cozy" Screening Room, which Collins described to him as

> "an aesthetic bridge" that links the silent film era with digital state-of-the-art. And while the 201-seat theater itself reflects this 80-year connection, the addition's hallways, vestibule, and even its restrooms have some of that old-time movie splendor.[9]

Within a month, the wisdom of building a second screen became apparent. Film revenues during the Screening Room's first 30 days of operation were almost double those of the previous month: The historic theater reported $16,164.25 in ticket sales; the Screening Room brought in $13,703.50.

REMAINING RESTORATIONS

With the annex open for business, attention turned to the remaining restoration of the historic theater, following plans that had been mapped out at the beginning of the capital campaign. First on the "must be done" list was the heating, ventilation, and air conditioning system. There had been no improvements to the system since 1956, and except for the entry foyer, the theater had never been air-conditioned. "The deterioration of paint and plaster due to moisture damage from humidity," Scott Clarke

THE 1950S MARQUEE. MT

stated in a memo, "is such that we cannot afford to 'restore' any more of the decorative surfaces until this problem has been dealt with." In November 1999, Ann Arbor-based Robertson-Morrison Inc. began installing a new HVAC system that would provide true air conditioning to the entire historic theater and greatly improve air flow and temperature control.

One month later, restoration contractor O'Neal Construction began work on the historic theater's façade and outer lobby, which had been dramatically altered in 1956 with the construction of a false drop ceiling. Decorative plasterwork would be uncovered and damage to it repaired. Mirrored and paneled walls would also be uncovered and carpeting removed from the original terrazzo floor. The jarringly modern glass doors installed across the front of the theater and at the entrance to the grand foyer were replaced and historically appropriate plenums were created to hide ductwork for the new air conditioning.

Work on the façade involved removing the triangular marquee erected in the 1950s and replacing decorative motifs that had been removed in 1956; ultimately a new vertical sign would be installed where the original had been located. This part of the restoration met some public resistance. When representatives from the Michigan Theater appeared before the Ann Arbor Historic District Commission to get permission to remove the triangular

Throughout most of the 1990s, the Michigan had competition from the State Theater's two screens a few doors east on State Street, and from the Ann Arbor 1 & 2 theaters on Fifth Avenue.

marquee, a few commission members and some local residents objected, arguing that the 1950s marquee and façade treatment were good examples of the architectural styles of their era and should be left alone, and that the lobby's marble and mirrors should be preserved.

In its account of the hearing, *The Ann Arbor News* reported that "Joe Tiboni, who presented 71 signatures to the commission from people who want the façade to stay, … called the box office 'an absolute gem' that should be saved. 'I would argue you'd at least want to preserve that box office as part of the history of the day.'"[10] Ultimately, the commission approved the removal of the marquee, the 1950s box office beneath it, and restoration of decorative motifs. In recognition of the historic importance of the 1950s marquee, theater staff salvaged from it a set of letters that spelled out "M-I-C-H-I-G-A-N" and mounted it on a wall of the corridor leading to the Screening Room.

The capital campaign had raised $4.8 million by the time the Screening Room opened. To pay for the work on the outer lobby and façade, an additional $600,000 was raised. Eventually the fundraising targets were increased again, to $6.4 million, to pay for completion of balcony décor and reinstallation of the vertical sign, completing the restoration.

NEW LANDSCAPE FOR DOWNTOWN FILM EXHIBITION

With the Michigan Theater's shift to a focus on film programming after its artistically ambitious Serious Fun! Series and Drama Season programs fell short at the box office, the University Musical Society gradually added live theater and contemporary performing arts to its long established classical music schedule and occasionally used the Michigan Theater as a presentation venue.

When the Michigan was approached in early 1996 about taking over the operation of the State Theater, Russ Collins pointed out to the board the advantages to such an arrangement: It would give the Michigan a monopoly on art-house cinema in Ann Arbor.

Throughout most of the 1990s, the Michigan had competition from the State Theater's two screens a few doors east on State Street, and from the Ann Arbor 1 & 2 theaters on Fifth Avenue. The latter were owned by the Goodrich chain, which bought the Fifth Forum Theater in 1979 and divided it into two small, narrow venues the next year. The "1 & 2," which screened mainly foreign and independent domestic features and were in direct competition with the Michigan Theater for films, closed in 1998 when Goodrich built the Quality 16 multiplex on Jackson Road. At that time, an offer from Goodrich to sell the "1 & 2" was met with little interest by the Michigan.

But an offer to operate the State Theater came about the same time and was greeted with considerable enthusiasm by the board of directors and the Michigan staff. The State had been divided into four screens in 1979 by its original owner, W.S. Butterfield Theatres Inc., and was sold in 1984 to Kerasotes Theatres. The theater steadily deteriorated under Kerasotes management, and in February 1989 was purchased by Hogarth Management, a real estate firm owned by the original Borders Bookshop co-founder, Tom Borders. Hogarth restored the building's historic art deco marquee and returned the main floor to a single retailing space, which was soon occupied by Urban Outfitters. The two screens on the second floor were reopened in 1992 as a second-run venue operated by Aloha Entertainment Inc., based in Canton, Michigan, and owned by B.W. and Billie Sperlin.

Over the next five years, the State Theater was only marginally success-ful. The two theaters, carved from the balcony of the original theater, were less than ideal venues. The screens sat at an odd, uncomfortable angle to the seats, there were no masks around the screens' borders, and sound spilled over from the adjacent theater and the ground floor store. Still, discount-movie customers patronized the theater in just sufficient numbers to keep the doors open.

When the Michigan was approached in early 1996 about taking over the operation of the State theater, Russ Collins pointed out to the board the advantages to such an arrangement: It would give the Michigan a mo-nopoly on art-house cinema in Ann Arbor and, with favorable lease terms, the State's business might be profitable as well. There were, however, some disadvantages. Taking over the State might distract the Michigan staff and boards at just the time when the capital campaign and new construction needed their attention.

Collins suggested that the best arrangement would be for the State Theater to contract for the Michigan Theater's services and not involve the Michigan in a lease at all. He was confident that the Michigan, with its

HELGA HOVER'S "STORE"
FOR PATRONS. MT

experience operating a theater as well as promoting films, would improve the State's business and allow it to operate more profitably than Aloha, and that a four-screen package – two at the State plus two, eventually, at the Michigan – would be appealing to distributors. The Michigan and State would no longer be competing with one another, giving the combination a considerable programming advantage.

In July 1997, the State Theater was purchased by a consortium of investors (some of whom had a strong interest in seeing the Michigan Theater succeed) that formed the State Theater LLC. In November, the Michigan Theater was hired to provide programming, marketing, and consultation services for the State Theater.

[1] Miramax resumed service to the Michigan later in the year.

[2] Klingelhofer, based in Oakland, California, had for many years worked in distribution and exhibition at Paramount Pictures Corp. and Twentieth-Century Fox before moving to the Landmark Theatre Corp. As Landmark's vice president for film buying, she was responsible for programming repertory calendars, first-run specialized and upscale commercial runs, genre series, and midnight shows in theaters across the United States. In 1992, Klingelhofer launched her own consulting service.

[3] Weiser served as the Bush administration's ambassador to Slovakia from 2001 to 2005. In 2009, he became chairman of the Michigan Republican Party.

[4] One of the houses, at 602 Washington Street, had been the home of Angelo Poulos and his family. His son, William Poulos, occupied it until the 1970s. At the time of Smokler's purchase the Cadillac Building housed a pair of women's clothing stores, but it had at one time been a Cadillac dealership.

[5] *The Ann Arbor News*, September 5, 1995: "Government aid to the arts is definitely going to decrease," Weiser told *The News*. "We have to put ourselves in position to be able to operate effectively without counting on any government help."

[6] In January 1996, the Michigan Theater Foundation applied for a $500,000 grant from the Towsley Foundation. In recognition of the foundation's past grants and Margaret Towsley's personal generosity to the theater, the application contained a provision promising no further requests for funds.

[7] Upon receiving the award, Ron Weiser said: "The Kresge board looks to the level of support already garnered by the applicant. Our leadership donors have demonstrated how much the community values the Michigan Theater."

[8] *The Ann Arbor News*, October 2, 1999. In an article about the opening of the Screening Room, Russ Collins said the that vision for the interior was that it should "complement but not imitate" the aesthetics of the historic theater.

[9] Ibid.

[10] "Michigan Theater's Renovation on Schedule," *The Ann Arbor News*, August 16, 1998.

An Award-Winning Community Center for the Arts

The opening of the Screening Room in October 1999 was a turning point in the history of the Michigan Theater. With another theater available for film showings, the historic theater could be freed up for large-scale events and community performing arts programs, film programming options were expanded, and the theater was better positioned to compete in the film exhibition market. By the end of 2000, the historic theater glowed anew with a carefully restored outer lobby and façade and, over the next two years, the balcony would be finished as well. From the stage, the completed auditorium resembled the bejeweled surface of an inverted golden bowl.

The Michigan Theater's newly installed vertical "blade" sign was lit for the first time on November 1, 2002. The evening marked Russ Collins' 20th year as executive director and formally launched celebrations in advance of the theater's 75th anniversary on January 5, 2003. The anniversary observance officially began on October 23 with a 75-day program designed to mark each year of the theater's existence. On each of those 75 evenings, a staff member took the stage before the screening of the feature film to present a vignette that captured one year's highlights in films and stage shows, world and community news, special theater events, and in some cases, personal recollections. A printed version of each vignette was published in *The Ann Arbor News*.

OPPOSITE: THE RESTORED FAÇADE. BY J. CLARK. MT

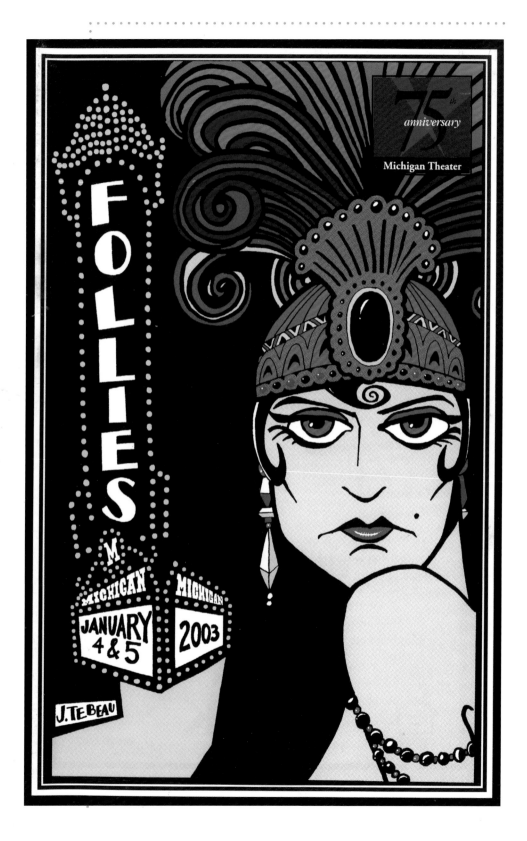

A pair of special events bracketed the anniversary observance. On October 23, theater organist Steve Ball accompanied a screening of the first film shown at the Michigan Theater, the lightweight and long-forgotten silent comedy *A Hero For a Night*. The film was preceded by a release party for the Michigan Theater's Christmas compact disc, *Under the Christmas Mistletoe*, which showcased the theater's organists performing on the Barton pipe organ.[1] Closing the celebration on January 4-5, 2003, was a concert staging of the Stephen Sondheim musical *Follies*. The show was chosen for its setting – a historic vaudeville theater, about to be torn down, that draws its former chorus girls and their stage-door Johnnies for one last reunion. The Michigan staging featured four members of the original Broadway cast plus Donna McKechnie, the Tony Award–winning musical theater star and a native of Royal Oak, Michigan; she was featured in a performance of the show business anthem *I'm Still Here*.[2]

ORGANIST STEVE BALL. MT

DIAMOND DUET

During its anniversary year, the Michigan Theater also entered into a partnership with the Ann Arbor Symphony to jointly celebrate its resident orchestra's own 75th birthday with three "Diamond Duet" productions. A "Masters of Movie Music" concert was scheduled for November 2003 and a "Best of Broadway" concert tribute to theater benefactor and former Michigan Theater Foundation chairwoman Judy Rumelhart was set for February 22, 2004. The third, a concert production of Leonard Bernstein's *Candide* the following May, would feature Metropolitan Opera mezzo-soprano Frederica von Stade and a cast that included other opera and Broadway professionals, University of Michigan musical theater students, and U-M School of Music faculty.

The month that saw the symphonic tribute to the theater and its organ also saw the passing of local silent-film enthusiast Art Stephan, founder of the Ann Arbor Silent Film Society and a source of information about the genre for the Michigan Theater staff.

The "Masters of Movie Music" program included Aaron Copland's score for *The Red Pony*, Erich Korngold's suite from *The Adventures of Robin Hood*, and a suite by John Williams from *Schindler's List*. At a planning meeting, board of directors member Henry Aldridge argued that a "Masters of Movie Music" program would not be complete without attention to the theater's Barton organ and proposed that the Ann Arbor Symphony commission a short work for theater organ and orchestra. After some discussion, the committee – which also included Collins, orchestra conductor Arie Lipsky, and Mary Stefek Blaske, chief executive officer of the A2SO – decided to commission a full concerto for the occasion.

University of Michigan composer and keyboardist Michael Daugherty was offered the commission (fittingly, Daugherty's grandmother had been a pianist for silent movies and Daugherty had played a Wurlitzer pipe organ at a theater in his native Cedar Rapids, Iowa). Daugherty's compositions included *Dead Elvis*, for bassoon and chamber ensemble; *Metropolis Symphony*, inspired by Superman comics; *Rosa Parks Boulevard*, and *Route 66*. His piece for "Masters of Movie Music," the imaginative and lovely *Once Upon a Castle*, was inspired by the extravagant San Simeon estate of newspaper magnate William Randolph Hearst – the real-life model for Charles Foster Kane in Orson Welles' *Citizen Kane*.[3] Michigan Theater organist Steve Ball received a standing ovation for his performance of the solo on the Barton. In a letter to *The Ann Arbor News*, James R. Irwin praised the theater and the symphony "for throwing such a classy bash":

Not only were these two organizations commissioning a brand new work during a time when orchestras across the country are scaling back due to diminishing funds, they commissioned the first-ever concerto for theater organ and orchestra. For two Ann Arbor organizations to call upon an Ann Arbor–based composer to write this historical addition to the world's orchestral repertoire was the organization's anniversary gift to the audience and the Ann Arbor community.[4]

A year later, the Daugherty concerto was broadcast on the nationally distributed American Public Radio program *Pipedreams*. The broadcast, titled "Once Upon a Theater," highlighted the role of the Barton pipe organ in saving the Michigan Theater.[5]

The month that saw the symphonic tribute to the theater and its organ also saw the passing of local silent-film enthusiast Art Stephan, founder of the Ann Arbor Silent Film Society and a source of information about the genre for the Michigan Theater staff. For many years the society held a monthly screening of rare films – the Screening Room served as the society's venue for the last two years of Stephan's life – and the accomplished conductor, composer, and musician usually accompanied the showings on piano.

LEGENDS OF ROCK & ROLL

OCTOBER 11, 2005
BONNIE
RAITT
BETTER THAN EVER

MICHIGAN
THEATER

"Best of Broadway," a tribute to Rumelhart for her many contributions to the arts in Ann Arbor,[6] was emceed by Rumelhart's singing partner, J. Lawrence Henkel. The concert showcased a number of guest artists performing music of George and Ira Gershwin, Irving Berlin, Richard Rodgers, and others in classic arrangements that Rumelhart had commissioned during her years as a cabaret singer in New York. *Ann Arbor News* reviewer Roger LeLievre commented that

> the night's most touching performance was offered by Henkel and Rumelhart herself. In their "Remembering" medley, which opened and closed with lyrics from The Fantasticks' "Try to Remember," the duo showed just what a pair of seasoned theater pros can do. They played off each other perfectly, evoking nostalgia, humor and just the pure joy of performing together.[7]

LEGENDS OF ROCK AND ROLL

The autumn of 2004 brought the debut of the Legends of Rock and Roll series, approved by the board of directors in 2003 as part of a commitment to diversify the theater's live programming. In addition to bringing in top rock acts, the series was intended to tap into a newly identified audience of potential donors – those financially successful adults who had been drawn to the Michigan Theater because of its live performances of popular music.[8] The series debuted on October 6 with former Beach Boy Brian Wilson's "Smile" concert marking the 2004 release of an album recorded in 1966-67; a return appearance by bluesman B.B. King followed in December. In 2005, the series presented Bonnie Raitt, Elvis Costello, Todd Rundgren, and Joe Jackson; strong lineups continued into the middle of the decade. In addition to the Legends of Rock and Roll Series, events presented by Live Nation, University Musical Society, The Ark, and other organizations at the Michigan included performances by

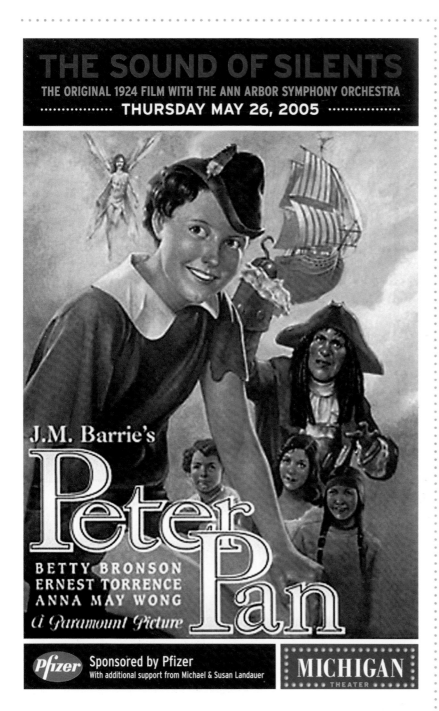

THE SOUND OF SILENTS

THE ORIGINAL 1924 FILM WITH THE ANN ARBOR SYMPHONY ORCHESTRA

THURSDAY MAY 26, 2005

J.M. Barrie's

Peter Pan

BETTY BRONSON
ERNEST TORRENCE
ANNA MAY WONG
a Paramount Picture

Pfizer Sponsored by Pfizer
With additional support from Michael & Susan Landauer

MICHIGAN
THEATER

Carly Simon, Leo Kottke, Jeff Tweedy, Philip Glass, Shawn Colvin, Jimmie
Dale Gilmore, Cyndi Lauper, Little Richard, Chick Corea, and Bela Fleck.
In May 2007, Peter Sagal brought *Wait, Wait, Don't Tell Me,* his popular
National Public Radio show, to the Michigan for a live taping.

THE RESTORED GRAND
FOYER MEZZANINE. CH

The theater's film program continued to screen a mix of new films, including *Hotel Rwanda*, *Downfall*, *Wild Parrots of Telegraph Hill*, *March of the Penguins*, *Grizzly Man*, *Good Night and Good Luck*, *Capote*, and *Brokeback Mountain*, and such classics as *The Adventures of Robin Hood*, *Dr. Strangelove*, *Creature From the Black Lagoon*, *The Godfather*, and *2001: A Space Odyssey*.

There were also silent features such as *The Black Pirate* and *The General*, and, in May 2005, a rare screening of the 1922 classic *Peter Pan* with a reconstruction of the original score conducted by Gillian Anderson. In 2006, Anderson returned to the Michigan to conduct the Ann Arbor Symphony Orchestra for a Criterion Collection recording of the score of the German silent film *Pandora's Box*.

Another goal of the Michigan Theater capital campaign was realized in May 2004 with the installation of the Ford Gallery of Ann Arbor Founders,[9] a collection of photographs and text mounted in 18 panels on the walls of the corridor leading from the historic theater to the Screening Room. The project was the brainchild of Del Dunbar, a local accountant and member of the Michigan Theater board of directors, and was executed by board member and Ann Arbor historian Louisa Pieper. The first set of narrative panels showcased the founders of Ann Arbor, the city's early settlers and its influential German immigrant community, business leaders and entre-preneurs, the arrival and growth of the University of Michigan, and the local impact of the abolition movement and the Civil War. A second set of panels explored broader themes such as the city's parks, schools, churches, theaters, and industry.

STRATEGIC PLAN

In the spring of 2004, the board of directors began to seriously address the marketing, programming, and fundraising goals set out in a strategic plan formulated by board Chairwoman Ruth Bardenstein. A manage-ment consultant, Bardenstein believed the theater needed a new and clear direction in the wake of its successful capital campaign and expansion. A top priority of the plan she developed was to implement a new corporate identity for the theater, including a new logo and a standardized appear-ance for all advertising and marketing communications. More broadly, her plan called for a renewed emphasis on the Michigan Theater as a film exhibitor by strengthening the theater's commitment to film not only as a stable and plentiful source of programming, but as the most eloquent of modern art forms.

Board members and staff were encouraged to think outside the "historic theater box" – to imagine how they might expand the mission of the theater into the neighborhood and community. Could this involve the development of an "arts corridor" stretching from the Michigan Theater to the State Theater, and might that include the Michigan Theater office building and perhaps a high-rise complex on the remaining site of the Cadillac Building? Should the board contemplate purchasing the State Theater if it became available? Should the theater become a more aggressive producer and pro-moter of live shows, or develop program outreach to minority communities in the city?

THE CITY HANDS OVER DEED
(L-R) JEAN ROWAN,
RUSS COLLINS, MAYOR
HIEFTJE. MT

The board of directors generally supported new initiatives that saw the theater as an anchor of the State Street business community, and envisioned a role for the theater as a leader in the arts for the downtown area. Minutes from a board meeting at the time show one member asking the board to envision opening a newspaper in 2014 to find a report that the "Michigan Theater owns State Theater, turned the Cadillac Building into the School of Performing Arts and used their ownership of the Michigan Theater office building as subsidy revenue."

For a model of how the Michigan could foster economic growth in the immediate area, the board looked to Cleveland's enormously successful Playhouse Square Center – four 1920s-era downtown theaters that were restored in the 1980s and '90s and attracted new business to downtown Cleveland. Should the Michigan Theater adopt a similar downtown development mission? Or, further afield, could the board consider operating the Madstone Theater? (Located in the Briarwood Mall, the multiscreen theater had been operated as an art house by a small commercial chain for about two years until it closed in June 2004.)

Despite the collapse of the real estate market in 2008, much actual development that was in the pipeline before the crash was under way in the immediate vicinity of the theater in 2007 and 2008.

Along these lines, the Michigan Theater leadership had the opportunity in 2004 to strengthen its relationship with the State Theater. For several years, the Michigan had been providing management advice to the State, scheduling its films and preparing its advertising. In August 2004, the State's owners asked the Michigan staff for an expanded managerial arrangement, which allowed for closer coordination of the theaters' activities. In response, the Michigan provided a separate staff and a schedule of films for the State.

In 2005, plans for a State Street-area development project gave the Michigan board a more specific opportunity to redefine the theater's wider role. Chicago-area developer Joseph Freed LLC was eyeing a parcel of land on Washington Street for a multistory retail and condominium project that included the Screening Room, the remainder of the Cadillac Building, and the houses on the block stretching to State Street. Representatives from Freed asked the board to consider what long-range needs the Michigan Theater might satisfy if additional space in the proposed development became available. During initial conversations, Collins and Albert Berriz, then chairman of the board of directors, expressed interest in about 53,000 square feet of space that could be considered for a range of uses – from additional office or screening space to a small theater for local dance and drama groups, or rehearsal and support space for the Ann Arbor Symphony Orchestra and similar groups.

Although discussed with great enthusiasm, none of these plans would become a reality after the real estate boom that encouraged such dreams went bust in late 2008. Nevertheless, the discussions led the board to address the fact that the foundation did not, in fact, own the Michigan

Theater: The deed still belonged to the city of Ann Arbor. To make clear to the community that the Michigan was truly independent and did not receive benefits as a city-owned asset, the board of directors in January 2005 formally asked the city to transfer the deed to the foundation itself.[10] In May 2007, the Ann Arbor City Council agreed to do so, and on January 4, 2008 – the theater's 80th anniversary – Ann Arbor Mayor John Hieftje handed the deed to Collins and board of directors Chairwoman Jean Rowan in a ceremony under the theater's marquee. Now, the Michigan Theater would be in a position to take advantage of any real estate development opportunities through a possible sale of the Cadillac Building.

Despite the collapse of the real estate market in 2008, much actual development that was in the pipeline before the crash was under way in the immediate vicinity of the theater in 2007 and 2008. The University of Michigan began construction of a student-housing facility on the site of the old Frieze Building – originally Ann Arbor High School – at the intersection of Washington and State streets. Nearby, McKinley Properties transformed the former TCF Bank building on Division Street between Washington and Liberty streets into the McKinley Town Centre, bringing in Google Adwords, Bar Louie, and other businesses. That project included construction of additional buildings east of the TCF site and would eventually involve renovation of the former National City Bank structure adjacent to the Michigan Theater. McKinley also relocated a historic house from Washington Street across from the Cadillac Building to build a high-rise apartment building at the northwest corner of Washington and Division streets. As the first decade of the new century drew to a close, the Michigan Theater was the center of what appeared to be a rapidly growing healthy and prosperous retail area. But in early 2011, the long-troubled Borders Group filed for Chapter 11 bankruptcy protection; that fall it decided to liquidate its remaining stores – including Borders Store Number 1, which stood directly across the street from the Michigan.

SUNDANCE ART HOUSE PROJECT

The Michigan Theater's selection to participate in the Sundance Institute's Art House Project was signal confirmation of its stature as a nationally important film venue. Created to celebrate the 25th anniversary of the nonprofit institute that promotes independent filmmaking, the project pays tribute to art-house theaters nationwide and chose 12 of

The Michigan Theater's selection to participate in the Sundance Institute's Art House Project was signal confirmation of its stature as a nationally important film venue.

those – including the Michigan – to exhibit a 25-year retrospective series of independent films.[11] The project became instrumental in creating a national organization of independent cinemas and would develop a broader, more dynamic role that included a film tour and a Sundance Film Festival-programmed series of short films, in which the Michigan Theater regularly participates.

Collins has served as co-chairman of the Art House Project since 2007. "It has been gratifying," he said in 2008, "to see the Art House Project evolve into a national movement … that I believe will dramatically grow audiences for art-house cinema."[12]

As motion picture technologies shifted from film to video, the Michigan Theater frequently upgraded its projection capabilities. In 2006, a grant from the Ann Arbor Downtown Development Authority and the State Street Area Association enabled the theater to purchase high-quality video projectors for both the historic theater and the Screening Room as well as several video screens for both lobbies. In the summer of 2009, the theater installed a high-definition digital 3-D video projector and presented a highly successful run of the Pixar film *Up!* in the historic theater. The theater could now project 16-, 35-, and 70-millimeter film as well as high-definition digital video.

These technical capabilities helped to further the Michigan Theater's reputation as an important film exhibitor. In April 2006 the theater hosted the first of what would become an annual Jewish Film Festival; in 2007 it was the site of a Polish Film Festival. In February 2007 the theater hosted metro Detroit's official Oscar Night America Party, a benefit sanctioned by the Academy of Motion Picture Arts and Sciences. *The Detroit News* reported:

With limousines, a red carpet and paparazzi, and WXYZ-TV personality Diana Lewis taking the stage in a stunning ball gown and borrowed jewels, Detroit's official Oscar Night America party was the next best thing to being there. An estimated 300 people, many in black-tie attire, braved the weather to attend the gala that benefits Illitch Children's Charities and the Michigan Theater in Ann Arbor. Sanctioned by the Academy of Motion Picture Arts and Sciences, the charity gala, held at the notable theater, was the only official Oscar viewing party in Michigan, one of 49 similar galas held across the country on Oscar Night.[13]

The theater also appeared consistently in local and regional "best of" lists. The Michigan was voted Best Independent Theater in the 2007 WDIV-TV "Vote 4 the Best" poll ("The Michigan has the most diverse programming of any theater in Michigan," commented one voter),[14] and consistently ranked as Best Movie Theater in *The Ann Arbor News* Readers' Choice awards.

Commenting on the 2007 Readers' Choice award, Collins observed that for the last 15 years or so, I think that the Michigan Theater has had the two dynamics of computers. There's the hardware and the software. ... As a piece of hardware – people respond extremely strongly to it, because it's a restored, historic theater. It's a slice of the past, and it's intrinsically beautiful. But you also have to have the software to make it something that usable. And so the program of films that we're able to offer in this community keeps the hardware enlivened and vital. The Michigan Theater is, bottom line, a community project, so to know that the community supports the theater, in terms of thinking of it as the best place to see a movie, is absolutely critical. It's so gratifying. The only reason we're here is for the community. And it's the only way we survive is through the community.[15]

OUTSTANDING HISTORIC THEATRE

As the Michigan Theater approached its 80th anniversary, it stood as a fully restored historic movie palace, equipped with an adequate stage and extensive film and digital projection capabilities. The theater's exterior, with its distinctive sign and brilliantly lit marquee, has become an iconic representation of Ann Arbor. It is open 365 days a year to present a diverse menu of film and music programming, and provides a home for lectures, conferences, weddings, and other special events.[16] By all measures the Michigan Theater has become one of the most successful examples of movie-palace

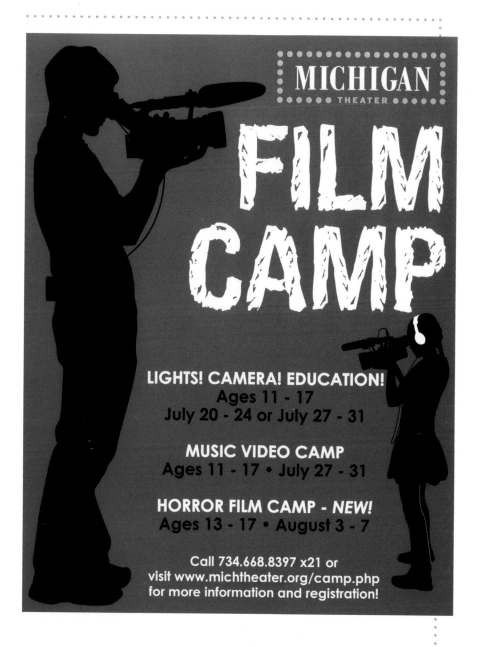
restoration coupled with ambitious programming and responsible fiscal management.

Of all the recognition it has earned in the early years of the new century, nothing marked more clearly the achievements of the theater's staff, trustees, volunteers, and members than the theater's selection by the League of Historic American Theaters as the winner of its Outstanding Historic Theatre Award for 2006.

The League of Historic American Theaters (LHAT) was formed in 1976 in Baltimore, and played a crucial role in the preservation of historic theaters around the country. The Michigan Theater has been a member of LHAT since 1983, and Collins has been active in the organization's leadership. Collins told *The News:*

> I see (the award) as something that the whole community should share in, because the Michigan Theater is indeed a community project – starting back in 1979, when the visionary folks stepped up to save the theater, and then all the boards and volunteers that have worked to make the Michigan Theater viable over the last nearly 30 years. …When you get a national award like this, I think that it validates the vitality of Ann Arbor – the vision that there is for our community, and the tremendous support and resources that are available in our community that allow us to operate on this very high level. [17]

When Collins accepted the award at a Hollywood ceremony, he not only represented present staff and board members, but also Angelo Poulos, Gerry Hoag, Paul Tompkins, John Hathaway, Ben Levy, and a host of other volunteers; and all the men, women, and children who over the past 80 years have walked through the Michigan Theater's doors to see a movie, attend a concert, savor the best popcorn in town, or just to relax for a few hours.

As Michigan Theater supporter Jerry Hartweg put it, in October 2007:

> Ann Arbor's Michigan Theater takes you back to the golden age of movies. The atmosphere inside is truly magical, beginning with the Barton organ and the beautiful interior of the theater. When you enter the theater, you are popped right back to 1928, and when the movie begins, you settle back and escape the problems of the world, at least for a little while. [18]

Those words are a fitting tribute to the Michigan Theater, since 1928 Ann Arbor's home for fine film and the performing arts.

[1] *Under the Christmas Mistletoe* was recorded in the summer of 2002 by Ann Arbor's Brookwood Studios, which was owned by theater volunteer David Lau. Sold at the customer service desk in the lobby of the Michigan, the CD was produced by Henry Aldridge and featured Aldridge, Steve Ball, Steve Warner, John Lauter, Newton Bates, Wade Bray, and Scott Smith performing Christmas selections that included a medley of carols by University of Michigan graduate Alfred Burt. The CD's title song was composed by Radio City Music Hall chief organist Dick Leibert.

[2] The four original cast members – Kurt Peterson, Marti Rolph, Harvey Evans, and Virginia Sandifur – played youthful, ghost-like reflections of the middle-aged leads in the 1970 Broadway production of *Follies*. In the Michigan concert production, they took the corresponding middle-aged roles of the youthful characters they originated. The production also featured students from the University of Michigan's Musical Theater Program and School of Music faculty members Martha Shiel and George Shirley; the orchestra was conducted by U-M faculty member Bradley Bloom, and Brent Wagner, director of the Musical Theater Program, was stage director. Emily Sutton-Smith, director of programs at the Michigan Theater, was instrumental in drawing the original cast members to Ann Arbor. She had studied voice in New York with Peterson, one of the youthful "ghosts" in the original 1970 production, and contacted him about plans for the show. Delighted with the prospect of playing the adult version of his character 31 years later, he approached other members of the cast.

[3] The first movement, "The Road to San Simeon," is suggested by the drive leading to the castle itself and opens with foreboding chords from the organ that suggest Bernard Herrmann's score for *Citizen Kane*. The second movement, "Silent Movies," is a lighthearted portrait of film actress and Hearst mistress Marion Davies. The third movement, "Neptune's Pool," was inspired by San Simeon's garden pool; the fourth movement, "Rosebud," of course refers to the name of Charles Foster Kane's childhood sled.

[4] *The Ann Arbor News,* December 9, 2003.

[5] *Pipedreams,* produced by Michael Barone in Minneapolis for American Public Radio, also aired selections from theater organist Steve Ball's *Having a Ball* CD and recordings of historic performances on the Barton organ from the 1960s. Michigan Theater Development Director Gayle Steiner "called me up," Barone recalled in an October 2004 interview with the author. "I am sure she remembered listening to *Pipedreams* when it could be heard on WUOM, put two and two together and thought I might be interested in the new Daugherty concerto.…

[I] spent the afternoon with Henry Aldridge and Gayle at the theater and got the feel of the place. I liked the idea of a bunch of guys getting together and making the Barton fully functional again after a period of decline, then confronting the horror of possible urban redevelopment. It is a marvelous story. It speaks to the power of music, I guess."

[6] In addition to her service as chairwoman of the Michigan Theater Foundation and head of the Michigan's first capital campaign, Rumelhart led the renovation effort for the University of Michigan's Hill Auditorium. As a producer of Stephen Sondheim's *Sweeney Todd* on Broadway, Rumelhart shared a Tony Award in 1979.

[7] Roger LeLievre, "Symphony Pays Tribute to a Classic," *The Ann Arbor News*, February 23, 2004.

[8] To encourage underwriting, series manager Lee Berry created a Backstage Club program that rewarded donors with excellent seats at three series concerts, a pre- or post-concert reception, a backstage pass, and a Michigan Theater premium membership.

[9] The gallery was funded in part by a $150,000 grant from the Ford Motor Company.

[10] In a letter to Ann Arbor Mayor John Hieftje dated January 15, Berriz and Collins argued that "not having standing as the owner handicaps the foundation's effectiveness in operating the Michigan Theater. The Foundation cannot use the Michigan Theater as collateral for bank loans…, city ownership is an impediment to many donors who feel that since the city owns the building, the city should also provide for its maintenance and care the way it must take financial responsibility for other city-owned properties. … The Michigan Theater (with the exception of the long expired millages) did not and does not now receive direct or indirect benefits from city ownership whatsoever. … In requesting the transfer of title, we acknowledge the city's stake and interest in the theater by pledging, in perpetuity, to use the Michigan Theater only to support the original mission of preserving, restoring and operating the building to benefit the community and the arts. In this spirit we would happily consider restrictions to the deed that would return the Michigan Theater to the City of Ann Arbor if the Michigan Theater Foundation should for any reason dissolve and we would also consider accepting restrictions that would prevent us from selling the Michigan Theater for commercial use or altering the historic architecture of the theater without approval from the city."

[11] In 2009, six more theaters were added to the Sundance Art House Project.

[12] "Sundance Institute Expands Collaboration With Local Art Houses," Sundance Institute, November 25, 2008.

[13] "A Night to Remember," *The Detroit News,* February 26, 2007.

[14] "Vote 4 the Best" comment by movie theater voter Rick Cronn, WDIV-TV website, October 2007.

[15] *The Ann Arbor News,* December 5, 2007.

[16] One notable program is the University of Michigan School of Art and Design's Penny W. Stamps Distinguished Speaker Series. Since 2003, established and emerging artists and designers have been appearing on the theater's stage each Thursday of the academic year.

[17] *The Ann Arbor News,* July 23, 2006.

[18] "Vote 4 the Best," WDIV-TV website, October 2007.

GERRY HOAG

Gerry Hoag (1900-1984) is the person whose name is most frequently associated with the history of the Michigan Theater. Hoag was the theater's manager from the day it opened its doors in January 1928 until his retirement in January 1974. He was also in charge of all Butterfield operations in Ann Arbor and responsible for managing all aspects of the company's local venues.

Hoag's career spanned an era in which local movie theater managers were often prominent civic leaders. Hoag was well known in the community and had close ties to University of Michigan administrators and city officials. He had a particular passion for the U-M football team and frequently corresponded with coaches.

A familiar figure on Liberty Street, Hoag often stood just under the marquee and greeted patrons in warm weather. Inside the theater, he would frequently sit in a comfortable chair that was strategically placed in the mezzanine of the lobby to give him a clear view of the front-of-house operations.

Hoag ran a tight ship at the Michigan. He was not above escorting unruly teenagers from the theater, but he possessed a wonderful sense of humor and his surviving letters reveal a warm, soft-hearted individual who loved family, sports, Ann Arbor, and especially the Michigan Theater.

Among the Hoag papers collected at the Bentley Historical Library at U-M is an undated letter (most likely from the late 1940s) from Mack Elementary School sixth-grader Mary Jo Harrington: "I found a dollar bill on Tuesday afternoon in the lobby and I have enclosed the money in the envelope. I did not know what to do with it."

OPPOSITE: GERRY HOAG
EXAMINES STATE THEATER
LOBBY DISPLAY. BHL

In the early 1920s, before radio sets were common household items, Hoag arranged to recreate U-M football games for students who attended shows at the Majestic.

Hoag's reply reads:

I am returning the dollar bill you found in the Michigan Theater lobby, as we have not been able to find the rightful owner. It was certainly thoughtful of you to take the time and the trouble of returning it to us by mail. I am enclosing three passes to the Michigan and three passes to the State so that you can invite your father and mother to be your guests at each of these theaters.

Hoag's wry humor comes through in notes to colleagues at the Butterfield central office in Detroit, also among the Bentley papers. On one occasion, he was chided for having misspelled the name of a Michigan Theater janitor on a payroll list. He replied:

Just because I spell it as ATKINS for 13 years doesn't mean I can't spell it AKTINS once in a while. It is simply NOT my fault. The typewriter joined the union back in 1923, and is just now showing its power. The keys keep jumping around smoethnig awful. My best – just don't run out of red ink on my account.

Hoag was born in Kalamazoo, Michigan in 1900 and began working for W.S. Butterfield Theatres Inc. in 1915 as an usher at a Saginaw theater, where he made 50 cents a day. Soon, he was promoted to a traveling treasurer for the company and later worked as a company auditor in Saginaw.

Hoag came to Ann Arbor in 1919 to manage the Majestic Theater, at 347 Maynard Street (where a parking garage now stands), where he booked films as well as some stage acts. Among them was an appearance by Jack Benny, who in the 1920s was a star on Broadway but, apparently, not known enough in the Midwest to fill many seats at the Majestic. For a story in 1944, Hoag told *The Ann Arbor News:*

(L-R) VAN JOHNSON,
JEAN HOAG, GERRY HOAG.
BHL

When Benny walked onto the stage and saw the sparse gathering before him, he wisecracked, "Something's wrong; I gave out more passes than this." Then he sat down on the footlights, invited the small turnout to move forward "like we was all out in the kitchen at home," and proceeded to enjoy himself and entertain the orchestra and house staff with a distinct variation of his act.

Benny returned to Ann Arbor over Thanksgiving weekend of 1929 to emcee *Tanned Legs,* a musical revue at the Michigan Theater. Hoag told *The News* in 1969 that

Jack was getting $1,500 a week but this was nothing, because he spent it all on the horses. While he was here, he went to the cigar store next door and placed $500 on a horse. When he came on stage that night, he walked on tearing up the ticket. He had lost. I gave him $500 to get to Chicago. It was at the Majestic Theater in Chicago that he signed a radio contract and made all of that money. He makes out he is the biggest tightwad in history, but really he was the easiest touch in show business.

Because it was near the U-M campus, the Majestic was popular with university students and frequently the scene of good-natured "demonstrations." On occasion, students would gather outside the theater after a football pep rally and demand free admission. After a few mild protestations Hoag always obliged, and the students loved him for it. Hoag recalled these incidents in a 1969 interview with Norman Gibson of *The Ann Arbor News:*

Somehow over the years, the impression has grown that these demonstrations followed football games. This is not true. They came after the pep rallies, usually at the Michigan Union, the night before the games. The only time one actually happened after a game was when the team came in from a successful game with Wisconsin. It was on a Sunday and at about 4 o'clock they came trooping down.

The biggest disturbances followed "cap night" in the spring. Anyone who remembers "cap night" has to be way on the other side of the generation gap, for this goes back to the day when university freshmen, or "frosh" as they were known in those days [the 1920s] wore little skull caps – they were made to wear them – called "pots." In the spring term, the sophomores and upperclassmen built a big fire in what was known as "the hollow," which was by the University Hospital, and the frosh were allowed to throw their pots into the fire.

Rushes on the theater weren't really the results they wanted. There was no confrontation – they were allowed to see the picture, and that was it. This took away half the fun.

In the early 1920s, before radio sets were common household items, Hoag arranged to recreate U-M football games for students who attended shows at the Majestic. He would rent a teletype line connecting the Majestic to an operator at the stadium. Hoag would read the plays from the teletype and describe them dramatically while moving a football around a miniature field set up on the Majestic's stage. If the team took a timeout or the line went down, Hoag would invent a few plays until things got going again. Once, before a packed theater, a teletype operator kept cutting into the line that connected the Majestic to an away game, creating great gaps in Hoag's coverage. "We never missed a play, though," Hoag told Gibson. "I called many a play – 'they're punting now … they're completing a pass …,' and so on – without having any idea of what was going on. I knew that if I had announced what had happened, I would have had 1,000 screaming and irate students on my hands."

As the popularity of radio grew in the 1920s, Hoag capitalized on it to attract patrons to the Majestic. On one occasion, Detroit radio station WWJ aired a talk by U-M football coach Fielding Yost and Hoag wanted the Majestic to present the broadcast. He enlisted a U-M professor to set up a receiving set and speakers at the theater, which was packed for the Yost radio talk. Hoag took the stage to explain the transmission process. "You see that single wire running up the stage?" he said. "That's the aerial." The audience, Hoag said, began to boo. "I suddenly realized," he recalled, "that they didn't believe me. They had seen outdoor antennas, but they just would not believe that one could work indoors."

As a passionate fan of U-M athletics, Hoag was in the habit of giving free passes not only to the entire football team, but also to individual players who scored touchdowns or otherwise distinguished themselves during games.

By 1928, radio had become so popular that on weeknights, Hoag regularly delayed the start of the Majestic's 7 p.m. movie by 15 minutes to allow patrons to listen to *Amos 'n Andy* from a radio the manager set up on the theater's stage.

Perhaps Hoag's most famous story from his days as the Majestic's manager was his discovery of Fred Waring, the bandleader (and financial backer for the Waring Blendor), at the 1922 Junior Hop at U-M's Waterman Gymnasium. Two popular bands had been booked for the J-Hop, an annual ballroom dance sponsored by the U-M junior class, and Waring's unknown ensemble was there as a backup. When Waring's band began to play, students stopped dancing and gathered around to listen. Hoag, who had come over from the Majestic to check out the event, was so impressed with the band's sound and popularity that he booked Waring's ensemble to play the Majestic for a four-day gig starting the following Sunday. Waring's band orchestra alternated with film screenings for three one-hour shows a day – and all the performances were sold out. "It was the orchestra's first theater performance, and it wasn't its last, either," Hoag told *The Ann Arbor News* in 1978. Waring never forgot the boost that he got in Ann Arbor and often worked "Hail to the Victors" into his college-song medleys; Hoag and Waring kept in touch and had the opportunity to visit again when the bandleader and his Pennsylvanians played at Hill Auditorium in the late 1970s.

In 1950, Hoag's connection to Waring came in handy when friends of Michigan Sen. Arthur H. Vandenberg wanted to arrange a performance of "The Whiffenpoof Song" on *The Fred Waring Show*, which was televised Sunday afternoons on CBS. Vandenburg had been diagnosed with cancer and, after several surgeries, managed to return briefly to the Senate floor in May 1950. Vandenburg's wife died in June and in the fall of that year he returned to his hometown of Grand Rapids.

According to a 1972 account in Gibson's "At This Stage" column in *The Ann Arbor News*, Hoag telephoned Waring and asked him to perform the song for the ailing senator. Waring replied that the week's show was already "timed down to the second. If we changed anything now, we'd have to start all over. But let me see what I can do." When Waring called back, he told Hoag that he'd raised the issue with Charles E. Wilson, president of the show's sponsor, General Electric; Wilson agreed to pull all the commercials from the week's show to open time for the song. A letter from Vandenburg following the show was one of Hoag's prized possessions. "I am hastening to thank you for one of the nicest things that ever happened to me," the senator wrote.

As a passionate fan of U-M athletics, Hoag was in the habit of giving free passes not only to the entire football team, but also to individual players who scored touchdowns or otherwise distinguished themselves during games. In early 1969, *The Michigan Daily*, U-M's student newspaper, published an article that exposed the practice of regular discounts to athletes from Hoag and other local merchants. The favors were in violation of NCAA rules, and the article sparked an investigation.

Hoag dismissed the criticism. "Why, I also give free tickets to the wonderful Michigan marching band, and to policemen, and to the Glee Club, and, hell, even to the staff of *The Michigan Daily!*" he told the *Chicago Daily News* in February for an article about the controversy. In April, Hoag wrote to William R. Reed, commissioner of athletics for the Big Ten Conference:

> Because I have given out passes for special endeavors by students at the University for nearly 50 years, I am mighty unhappy for the situation. … To let the pseudojournalists at *The Michigan Daily* do harm to our clean and well-regulated athletes raises my hackles. … [E]verything for the [last] 50 years has always been above board. Have you any ideas? I hate like heck to stay this frustrated.

In his reply later that month, Reed expressed sympathy and promised a swift clarification of NCAA rules. Reed, who had gone to high school in Ann Arbor, also shared a boyhood memory in the letter:

> Dear Jerry: I address you so familiarly because of an acquaintance which you would not have reason to remember, but which for my part goes back 37 years. On Good Friday in 1932, as a high school student in Ann Arbor, I "crashed" the exit door of the Michigan Theater. You apprehended me and you gave me a lecture at the time, the lesson of which I think I have

In the late 1960s, Hoag became concerned about the changing obscenity standards for films and occasionally expressed his disapproval of language he heard in new releases.

retained through the years, and certainly value. You pointed out the difference between being "smart," which I thought I was being, and an intrusion upon others' property rights. The illustration was that a theater admission was in essence nothing different from a can of soup on a grocer's shelf and it was agreed that I would not think of walking into a grocery store and grabbing off that can of soup.

On June 16, Hoag received a letter from Marcus L. Plank at the U-M Law School along with a copy of the minutes from the Big Ten Joint Group meeting where the issue was discussed. The group ruled it permissible for "member institutions" to provide local movie tickets to athletes during the school year "provided the tickets are not made available in recognition of special achievements by individuals." In other words, Hoag was again free to give out passes.

In the late 1960s, Hoag became concerned about the changing obscenity standards for films and occasionally expressed his disapproval of language he heard in new releases. By then, the old Production Code censorship system had been replaced by a new rating system that permitted much more frank vocabulary in motion pictures. Hoag also witnessed the era's social unrest in Ann Arbor and vigorously protested when it affected the Michigan Theater. In mid-November 1969 Ann Arbor police officers were called to the theater, where they removed one person for causing a disturbance and were confronted by a crowd of about 20 youths in front of the theater. On November 30, police were called to the theater four times because a group of youths who called themselves "The Forty Thieves" or "The Jones School Gang" had shouted obscenities at theater patrons.

Hoag was indignant that city officials seemed unconcerned and that the incidents would not be prosecuted. In a draft of a letter to then-Mayor Robert Harris, Hoag wrote:

> I am … informed that there is no such thing as obscenity in Ann Arbor unless one subjected to it is held captive. As long as he or she can escape, there is no charge. Would you like to hear a dozen women who heard these hoodlums say "we'll kick the s--- out of you, you mother--------- son of a bitch"? This is not said back of a barn, but in a public place where they had no right to be. … And I am a bit fed up.

While he wrestled with cultural changes in movies and in the community, Hoag became something of a hero to academics and local groups. Recognizing his knowledge of film history, he was asked on several occasions to give talks to the Ann Arbor Rotary, to which he belonged. Hoag also became a popular guest lecturer for U-M film history classes. U-M film professor Robert E. Davis wrote Hoag on March 14, 1969:

> The thing my class does not get in their study of the history of the movies is a good idea of the distribution system and the business side of theatrical presentation. If you would be willing to talk about how films are distributed now, how they are chosen for various theaters, how the individual theater operator works with the distributor, this would contribute greatly to the class.

Hoag retired on January 5, 1974, the 46th anniversary of the opening of the Michigan Theater and after more than 50 years with the Butterfield organization; he was honored at the Michigan Theater's 50th Anniversary Show, in October 1978. Hoag died on April 30, 1984, leaving his wife, Jean; his daughter, Betty; and five grandsons. In an obituary the next day, *Ann Arbor News* writer Julie Wiernik recounted a number of incidents from his colorful career and the show business greats, including Jack Benny and Bing Crosby, who performed at the Michigan when he was its manager. The headline of the obituary referred to Hoag as Ann Arbor's "dean of movies."

All sources for Appendix A are found in the Gerald H. Hoag Papers, Box 1, Bentley Historical Library, The University of Michigan, Ann Arbor.

Founding Board Members of the Michigan Community Theatre Corporation, 1979

Henry Aldridge, *Michigan Theater organist and professor of speech and dramatic arts at Eastern Michigan University*

Newton Bates, *Michigan Theater organist and real estate agent*

Richard Bay, *University of Michigan Alumni Association*

Frank Beaver, *professor of speech communications and theatre, U-M*

Louis Belcher, *mayor of Ann Arbor*

Alan Billings, *professor of speech communications and theatre, U-M*

Charles Borgsdorf, *attorney*

John Briggs, *International Alliance of Theatrical Stage Employees*

John Carver, *Second Chance*

Grant Cook, *Motor City Theatre Organ Society*

Carl Daehler, *Ann Arbor Chamber Orchestra*

Jean Galan, *U-M Professional Theatre Program*

John Hathaway, *attorney*

Mary Hathaway, *Ann Arbor Historical Foundation*

Elwood Holman, *Colvin-Robinson Associates Inc.*

Robert L. Johnson, *certified public accountant*

Reuel Kenyon, *Ann Arbor Federation of Musicians*

Richard Lotz, *Ann Arbor Convention (Conference) and Visitors Bureau*

Peggy Magoon, *Ann Arbor Civic Ballet*

Gilbert Ross, *Ann Arbor Symphony Orchestra*

Charles Sutherland Jr., *Ann Arbor Civic Theatre*

Karen Young, *U-M Office of Major Events*

THE BARTON PIPE ORGAN

One of the elements making a visit to the Michigan Theater a unique experience is the magnificent Barton theater pipe organ, which is played before almost every film screening in the historic theater. Since its full restoration in 1972, the Barton has been in regular use for most public events at the theater including overtures before films, silent film accompaniments, Ann Arbor Symphony concerts, and special events.

The Michigan Theater's Barton pipe organ was installed in the fall of 1927 just before the theater's opening on January 5, 1928. It carries a factory Opus number of 245. There is some evidence that the builder had to make modifications to the instrument at the time it was installed because the main (house left) chamber was smaller than indicated on the building's blueprints. To make everything fit into this smaller space, the Barton technicians eliminated one set of pipes and moved the relay to a small room on the main floor of the theater rather than installing it in the left chamber.

Throughout the 1920s most motion picture theaters had pipe organs for the accompaniment of silent films and to play along with the resident orchestra. Michigan's W.S. Butterfield Theatres Inc. chain had a contract with the Barton Organ Company of Oshkosh, Wisconsin. Most of the organs provided for the Butterfield theaters were three-manual, ten-rank organs known as "Butterfield Specials." The instrument installed in the Michigan, however, is larger. It has a somewhat more powerful blower and three additional ranks: a posthorn, a solo string, and an oboe horn.

OPPOSITE: THE BARTON THEATER PIPE ORGAN, OPUS 245. CH

PAUL TOMPKINS. BHL

In addition, the Michigan Barton has a deluxe console with extra stop tabs and combination pistons. No one seems to know why this larger pipe organ was installed at the Michigan, but it could be that Butterfield executives wished to make an impression on Ann Arbor audiences, or perhaps manager Gerry Hoag insisted on a bigger instrument for the theater.

The Michigan's first organist was Barton employee Floyd Hoffman, who played during the theater's opening weeks in 1928. He was replaced in February 1928 by Harold Loring, who played until June. During the summer of 1928, organist W.A. Warner and theater orchestra member Thelma Feltis did the honors; and in September 1928 Bob Howland took over. Howland continued as the theater's organist until he was replaced by Paul Tompkins in April 1931.

Tompkins, of Jackson, Michigan, was just 25 when he arrived at the Michigan, but had already made a name for himself at the Loews Valencia Theater in Baltimore before returning to the state to attend the University of Michigan. Soon he was a local celebrity. An April 9, 1931, item in *The Ann Arbor Daily News* "Stage and Screen" column announced Tompkins' arrival in town, reporting that "the star organist of the Loew's Inc., string of houses in the east" was "noted for spontaneity of his keyboard performances":

> This will be a welcome diversion. In the first place, the Michigan has a really wonderful instrument in the Barton. In the second place, there isn't any combination of apparatus, effects, money, or all three that can give through a talkie screen speaker the true music of an organ well played. And we think Paul Tompkins is the man to find some hidden musical value in that organ.

Tompkins never accompanied silent films. He played theme-based programs – "Trip Around the World," "Football," "Thanksgiving," "Musical Christmas Tree" – consisting of popular songs with lyrics projected on the screen. *Ann Arbor Daily News* display advertisements from the early to mid-1930s suggest that he performed every day, although probably not for every show.

Tompkins' tenure at the Michigan Theater was interrupted by World War II, when he served in the U.S. Army. After his discharge in 1945, he returned to the Michigan and played on a fairly regular basis until May 1950, when he moved on and played the Hammond organ at the Weber's Supper Club on Jackson Road (later, the site of a car dealership). Tompkins performed at the Michigan for a few special occasions in the 1950s and early 1960s before retiring to the Caribbean; he died in 1974.

In those post-Tompkins decades, the organ was seldom played but protected by a blue canvas cover and Hoag's watchful eye. At some point in the 1960s, the instrument suffered water damage to the flute, tuba, and string chests located in the main (house left) pipe chamber. Dick Houghton of Milan did some repairs, replacing some damaged electro-pneumatics with direct electric actions. In the late 1960s, Motor City Theatre Organ Society member Dave Lau made several recordings on the organ during late-night visits to the theater. They reveal that the instrument sounded good even though not all of it was playing properly. In the spring of 1970,

Over the years, a few alterations were made to the organ but always with the intention of maintaining its historical authenticity.

Henry Aldridge initiated an effort to have the Barton completely restored and enlisted the aid of Ben Levy and fellow organ society members. They began work in February 1971 by cleaning and repairing pipes, releathering the combination action in the console, and fixing leaks.

In June 1972, the organ society presented a preview concert performed by Rick Shindell of Toledo, Ohio. The first formal concert, however, was in September 1972 by Lyn Larsen, who brought the glittering gold and red console up on its original Barton four-poster lift to the strains of *Hail to the Victors,* the U-M football fight song.

In December 1972 Rupert Otto played the first public film overture, to a screening of *The Poseidon Adventure.* Newton Bates and Aldridge soon joined him; the three continued to play before movie screenings on Friday and Saturday evenings until the theater closed as a commercial operation in August 1979. During this time, the Motor City Theatre Organ Society maintained and promoted the instrument, holding an open house on the second Sunday of each month that featured a guest artist and then "open console" time for anyone who wanted to play. The chapter also sponsored professional concerts and silent films throughout the 1970s.

Use of the organ resumed when films returned to a nonprofit Michigan Theater in September 1979. Bates and Aldridge continued to perform; Otto retired to North Carolina. Throughout the 1980s and 1990s a number of different organists regularly played the instrument, including Don Haller, Larry Kass, Victor Barz, Fred Vipond, Scott Foppiano, John Lauter, the Rev. Jim Miller, Scott Smith, Loren Greenawalt, the Rev. Andrew Rogers, and Jim Leaffe. Lauter and Leaffe often accompanied silent films, sometimes alone and at other times with orchestra. The instrument was also used occasionally by the Ann Arbor Symphony Orchestra to fill indicated organ parts in such compositions as Holst's *The Planets* and Respighi's *The Pines of Rome.*

Over the years a few alterations were made to the organ, but always with the intention of maintaining its historical authenticity. The original electro-pneumatic relay, combination action, and console layout were maintained in excellent condition and were not replaced by computer systems. The Barton four-poster lift, which raises the console out of the orchestra pit, is also original. The modifications include the addition of couplers and a few rank extensions. The most sonically noticeable of these changes is the addition of a bottom 16' octave of Diaphones. These add considerable power and definition to the organ's pedal division.

By 2008, the Barton organ was regularly played during the 30-minute interval between the opening of the theater and the beginning of the evening's first film. Aldridge, Bates, Steven Ball, Stephen Warner, Emily Seward, and Andrew Rogers were the house organists; Scott Smith of Lansing, Michigan, maintained the instrument; and Aldridge made out a monthly schedule for the organists.

The Michigan Theater is unique among historic theaters in that its pipe organ is used regularly and is maintained in excellent condition.

The staff organists for the Michigan Theater must have a considerable repertoire and flexible musical style, and be able to play for sometimes noisy and inattentive audiences for anywhere from five to 30 minutes, depending upon the needs of the theater. On a typical evening, the organist arrives at the theater at least 30 minutes before the movie is to begin and prepares the organ for the performance. Until the theater opens, the organist has a chance to make sure that the organ is working properly and even has the opportunity to practice for a few minutes.

Organists usually play an up-tempo "console raiser" while bringing the Barton up to full view on the lift, and alternate between fast and slow pieces for the rest of the set. They usually play for 20 to 30 minutes, until the projectionist signals them to stop with a buzzer and flashing light at the console.

Sometimes things can go wrong. On a few occasions the instrument has developed a note that sticks (known as a cipher); the only alternative to playing along with the stuck note is to turn the organ off and end the performance prematurely. Once, a power failure disabled the organ's electrical system while Rupert Otto was playing; on another occasion, a wayward bat swooped over Aldridge's head. Sometimes patrons get a bit unruly, especially after a football game, but most of the time the film's organ overtures go smoothly. Playing a theater pipe organ on a regular basis in the 21st century is a unique pleasure that is worth whatever occasional difficulty an organist might encounter.

The Michigan Theater is unique among historic theaters in that its pipe organ is used regularly and is maintained in excellent condition. The sound of the now iconic Barton creates an ambience that makes a visit to the theater very special.

STOP LIST FOR BARTON OPUS 245

PEDAL
Reading from Left to Right. One Bolster

Pedal Resultant	32'
Tibia Clausa	16'å
Bourdon	16'
Tuba	16'
Diaphone	16'
Diaphone	8'
Tibia Clausa	8'
Tuba	8'
Cello	8'
Flute	4'
Cymbals on Pedal	
Accomp to Pedal	8'
Trumpet	8'

ACCOMPANIMENT
Reading from Left to Right Lower Bolster

Vox Humana T.C.	16'
Clarinet T.C.	16'
Contra Viole	16'
Diaphonic Diapason	8'
Claribel Flute	8'
Tibia Clausa	8'
Oboe Horn	8'
Vox Humana	8'
Clarinet	8'
Tuba	8'
Kinura	8'
Viole D'Orchestra	8'
Viole Celeste	8'
Solo String	8'
Two blank tabs	

Reading Left to Right Upper Bolster

Accomp to Accomp	4'
Orchestral Flute	4'
Tibia Clausa	4'
Violin	4'
Viole Celeste	4'
Twelfth	22/3'
Flautino	2'
Marimba	

GREAT
Reading Left to Right on Lower Bolster

Trumpet T.C.	16'
Tibia Clausa	16'
Tuba	16'
Diaphonic Diapason T.C.	16'
Oboe Horn T.C.	16'
Vox Humana T.C.	16'
Clarinet T.C.	16'
Viole D'Orchestra T.C.	16'
Diapason	8'
Concert Flute	8'
Tibia Clausa	8'
Oboe Horn	8'
Vox Humana	8'
Clarinet	8'
Orchestral Oboe	8'
Tuba	8'
Kinura	8'
Trumpet	8'
Viole D'Orchestra	8'
Viole Celeste	8'
Solo String	8'
Great to Great	16'
Great to Great	4'

Reading Left to Right on Upper Bolster

Solo to Great	16'
Principal	4'

Flute	4'
Tibia Clausa	4'
Violin	4'
Viole Celeste	4'
Solo String	4'
Nazard	2 2/3'
Tibia Twelfth	2 2/3'
Piccolo (Tibia)	2'
Fifteenth	2'
Tierce	1 3/5'
Marimba Harp	8'
Chrysoglott	8'
Xylophone	8'
Cathedral Chimes	8'
Glockenspiel	4'
Orchestra Bells	4'
Three blank tabs	

SOLO
Reading Left to Right on Lower Bolster

Tibia Clausa	16'
Vox Humana T.C.	16'
Tuba	16'
Diaphonic Diapason	8'
Tibia Clausa	8'
Oboe Horn	8'
Vox Humana	8'
Orchestral Oboe	8'
Tuba	8'
Kinura	8'
Trumpet	8'
Solo String	8'
Viole D'Orchestra	8'
Two blank tabs	
Tibia Clausa	4'
Cornet	4'
Xylophone	8'
Cathedral Chimes	8'

Glockenspiel	8'
Orchestra Bells	4'
Four blank tabs	

SECOND TOUCH
PEDAL

Tuba	16'
Diaphone	8'
Bass Drum	
Snare Drum	
Cymbal	
Kettle Drum	
Thunder	

ACCOMPANIMENT

Trumpet	8'
Tuba	8'
Tibia Clausa	8'
Glockenspiel	4'
Triangle	
Solo to Acc.	8'

GREAT

| Tuba | 16' |
| Tibia Clausa | 8' |

TREMULANTS

Main
Solo
Tibia
Vox

TOE STUDS

Fire Gong
Siren
Steamboat Whistle
Auto Horn
Bird Song

EXPRESSION PEDALS
Left (Div. I)
Right (Div. II)
Master
Crescendo

SFORZANDO

COMBINATION PISTONS

ACCOMPANIMENT MANUAL
General Cancel
Seven Pistons
Manual Cancel

GREAT MANUAL
Seven Pistons
Manual Cancel

SOLO MANUAL
Five Pistons
Manual Cancel

INDICATOR LIGHTS
Sforzando
Crescendo
Blower On/Off

BUZZER TO BOOTH

BARTON LIFT LEVER

BLOWER ON/OFF

CONSOLE LIGHT ON/OFF

MAIN CHAMBER (left)
16'-2' Concert Flute
16'-4' Open Diapason
16'-4' Tuba
8' Clarinet
8'-2' Viole d' Orchestre
8'-4' Viole Celeste
Chrysoglott Harp (37 metal bars)
Bird Whistle

SOLO CHAMBER (right)
16'-2' Tibia Clausa
8' Vox Humana
8' Kinura
8' Oboe Horn
8' Orchestral Oboe
8' Solo String
8' English Posthorn

Marimba (37 notes)
Xylophone (37 notes)
Glockenspiel/Orchestra Bells (37 notes)
Cathedral Chimes (20 notes)
Cymbal
Tambourine
Castanets
Wood Block
Tom-Tom
Snare Drum
Bass Drum/Kettle Drum
Triangle
Auto Horn
Acme Siren
Steamboat Whistle
Bell
Fire Gong
7-1/2 HP Spencer blower
3 manual horseshoe console

ILLUSTRATION AND PHOTO CREDITS

BHL   Bentley Historical Library, The University of Michigan, Ann Arbor. All photographs are from the Gerald H. Hoag Papers, Box 1 except for page 80, which is from the W.S. Butterfield Collection, Box 1, and pages 5 and 16 which are attributed to the Bentley Historical Library.

MT   Michigan Theater Foundation Archives, Ann Arbor, Michigan

HBA   Personal collection, Henry B. Aldridge

CH   Christine Hoffman, photographer

All display advertisements are reproduced from back issues of The Ann Arbor News, on microfilm at the Graduate Library of The University of Michigan, Ann Arbor.

Index

Abington Theater (Detroit), 27

Adams, Gerry, 97

Adam's Rib, 59

Albee, Edward, 85

Aldridge, Henry, 93, 102, 104, A106-7, 186, 199n1, 200n5, 217, 219; and efforts to save the Michigan Theater, 112, 113-14, 115, 116, 118; as performer on the organ, 103, 151; and restoration of the Barton pipe organ, 98, 218; as theater volunteer, 119, 132, 147

Alexander, Bob, 147

Allen, Dennis M., 38

All the Brothers Were Valiant, 68

Amadeus, 141, 142, 152n3

American Theatre Organ Society, 101

Anderson, Gillian, 160, 166n7, 190

And God Created Woman, 74-75

Ann Arbor Blues and Jazz Festival, 159

Ann Arbor Chamber Orchestra, 143, 153n9, 160

Ann Arbor Civic Ballet, 67

Ann Arbor Civic Theatre, 140-41

Ann Arbor Film Co-op, 127-28

Ann Arbor Film Festival, 122

Ann Arbor, Michigan: development in, 194; founders of, 191; historic preservation in, 113, 176-77. See also Michigan Theater; State Theater

Ann Arbor Silent Film Society, 187

Ann Arbor Symphony Orchestra, 141, 153n9, 165, 185-87, 190, 218

Angell, James, 14n7

Arcade Theater, 6, 7, 15n18

Armstrong, Louis, 61

Astaire, Fred, 59

As Time Goes By, 151

Baden, Carla, 166n1

Balaban and Katz, 15n15

Ball, Steve, 185, 186, 199n1, 199n5, 219

Ballet Russe de Monte Carlo, 66-67, 78n2

Bardenstein, Ruth, 191

Bardot, Brigitte, 74-75

Barkleys of Broadway, The, 59

Barr, Richard, 85

Barrymore, Ethel, 8, 61

Barrymore, John, 8, 37

Barthelmess, Richard, 39, 46-47n10

Barton, Dan, 24

Barton Organ Co., 24, 215

Barton pipe organ (Michigan Theater), 21, 24, 44, 46n2, 85, 107, 187, 215-23; Christmas CD of performances on, 185, 199n1; performances on, 61, 98-99, 101, 102-6, 115, 118, 123, 219-20; restoration of, 97-100, 101-2, 218

Barz, Victor, 218

Bates, Newton, 103, 104, 118, 153n16, 199n1, 217, 219

Beatty, E. C., 24, 53, 54, 55-56

Beckerman, Richard, 124n1

Belasco, David, 9

Belcher, Lou, 114, 115, 117, 120, 122, 134, 135, 137n8, 146

Bennington, Charles, 34

Benny, Jack, 10, 41, 42, 43, 59

Berlin, Irving, 59

Bernstein, Leonard, 156, 157, 166n2, 185

Berriz, Albert, 170, 193, 200n10

Berry, Lee, 158, 166n6, 200n8

"Best of Broadway," 188

Bestor, Don, 43

Bijou, 3, 13, 14n6

Birth of a Nation, The, 9, 14-15n10, 121

Black Pirate, The, 144

Blackmer, Sidney, 78n7

Blackstone, Harry, 42

Blake, Eubie, 35

Blaske, Mary Stefek, 186

Bloom, Bradley, 109n6, 199n2

Bogart, Humphrey, 59

Bolcolm, William, 166n7, 174

Booth, Edwin, 8

Borders, Tom, 164, 178

Borgsdorf, Charles, 114

Bray, Wade, 199n1

Brenner, David, 156

Brief Encounter, 59

Briel, Joseph Carl, 9

Briggs, John, 119, 124-25n6, 136n4

Britton, Frank & Milt, 43

Brown, William, 62

Broxholm, Julia, 153n16

Burt, Alfred, 199n1

Burton, Richard, 68

Butterfield, W. S., 10, 12-13, 15n16, 24, 26

Butterfield Theatres Inc., 12, 15n12, 53, 82-83, 163-64, 204; and film censorship, 75-77; and the Michigan Theater, 19, 29, 49, 114-15, 116, 145; during World War II, 54-57

Cabin in the Sky, 59

Calman, Emil, 6

Cameron, Margaret, 146-47

Campus Theater, 72-73, 163, 164; censorship at, 74-77

Candide (Bernstein), 185

Capitol Theater (Detroit), 51
Capra, Frank, 72
Carroll, Harry, 2, 35
Carter, Gaylord, 101
Caryl, Frederick G., 92-93, 95n17, 106
Casino theater, 2, 3, 13
censorship, 74-77, 79n10, 79n13
Chadwick, Ida Mae, 24, 33
Chaplin, Charlie, 15n18, 59
Christmas Carol, A, 141, 165
Cinema Guild, 121
Cinemascope, 68, 87
Cinerama, 67
Circus, The, 15n18
Citizen Kane, 59
Clarke, J. Scott, 170, 175-76
Classic Film Theater (CFT), 128, 141, 144-45
Cliquot Club Eskimos, 43, 47n15
Collins, Russ, 187, 192; as co-chairman of the Art House Project, 195; as executive director of the Michigan Theater, 139-40, 141-43, 144-45, 151, 161-62, 169, 179-80, 183, 198, 200n10
Comic Opera Guild, 165
Concerts Excelsior, 128, 129
Confrey, Zez, 34
Connors, Irene, 106, 109n6
Cook, Barbara, 103, 112, 121
Cook, Grant, 103, 112, 113
Copland, Aaron, 186
Copperfield, David, 156
Costello, Elvis, 188
Crane, C. Howard, 51
Creature From the Black Lagoon, 70
Crosby, Bing, 59
Crying Game, The, 165
Cugat, Xavier, 49, 61

Daehler, Carl, 143-44, 153n10
Dames, Theodore, 29

Darwell, Jane, 59
Daugherty, Michael, 186087
Daughter of the Plains, A, 6
Davies, Valentine, 62
Days of Heaven, 118
Dell, Helen, 101
Derek, John, 70-71, 78n7
Dewhurst, Colleen, 161
Dial M for Murder, 70
"Diamond Duet" productions, 185-88
Disney, Walt, 41
Dobson, Russell, 6
Don Juan, 37, 142, 143-44, 152-53n8
Douglas, Lloyd C., 68
Douglas, Paul, 61
Dunbar, Del, 191

Easter Parade, 59
Eaton, Charles, 38
Eberson, Drew, 87
Eberson, John, 87
Edison, Thomas Alva, 1
Ellington, Duke, 49
Evans, David, 153n12
Evans, Harvey, 199n2
Evita, 142-43, 152n5

Fader, Lester, 86
Fantasia, 59
Feltis, Thelma, 216
Ferrer, Jose, 59
Field, Betty, 209
Fifth Forum, 86, 88, 95n9
Film Flam, 66, 78n1
Finkel, Maurice, 19, 27, 29
First National/Warner Brothers, 12, 15n15
Fischer, Ken, 140, 143
Fleet's In, The, 50
Flying Karamazov Brothers, 161, 167n9
Follies, 185, 199n2
Foppiano, Scott, 218
Ford, Jim, 104

Ford, John, 59
Ford Gallery of Ann Arbor Founders, 191
Fort Ti, 69
Fox Film Corp., 12, 38
Fox Village Theater, 86-87, 88, 90
Foy, Eddie, 46n3
Foy Family, 35
Frank, Richard C., 132, 137n6, 149, 153n12
Freed, Joseph, 193
Freganza, Trixie, 35
Frenza, Jim, 113
Friends of the Michigan Theater, 113-14, 124n2
Fulbright, J. William, 70

Galliard Brass Ensemble, 153n16
Garland, Judy, 59
Garson, Greer, 59
Gehring, Lola, 67
Ghost Talks, The, 38
Gibson, Norman, 99, 108n4, 206-7
Gies, Julie, 135
Gilbert and Sullivan, 84-85, 94n3
Girl of the Golden West, The, 9
Glass, Philip, 156, 157, 161
Goldcoast Theater (Detroit), 27
Gottschalk, Louis F., 160
Gowthorpe, M. F., 82
Grandberg, Lois, 24
Great Train Robbery, The, 1
Greenawalt, Loren, 218
Greene, Earl W., 114
Grenzebach, John, 133-34
Griffith, D. W., 9, 39, 160
Guthrie, Arlo, 108n5
Guthrie, Tyrone, 84-85, 94n3

Hagen, Uta, 59
Hall, Mordaunt, 46n10
Haller, Don, 218
Hamblin Opera House (Battle Creek, Michigan), 12

Hanley, Bo, 103, 121, 130
Hanley, Robert, 103
Harrington, Mary Jo, 203-4
Harris, Robert, 212
Hart, Kitty, 14n2
Hartweg, Jerry, 198
Hathaway, John, 113, 114
Hathaway, Mary, 113
Haven, Jim, 130
Hayes, Helen, 8
Hellzapoppin, 58
Henkel, J. Lawrence, 188
Henry, Eugene, 14n2
Henry Boyle Theater (Fond du Lac, Wisconsin), 12
Hero for a Night, A, 24, 31n13, 185
Herrick Foundation, 167n14
Herrmann, Bernard, 199n3
Hieftje, John, 192, 194, 200n10
Hills of Strife, The, 6
Hill's Opera House, 8
Hilton Sisters, 35
Hines, Earl "Fatha," 61
Hitchcock, Alfred, 59, 84
Hoag, Gerald, 44, 45, 94-95n8, 103, 106; and Jack Benny, 10, 41, 204-5; death of, 212; early career of, 204; as manager of the Majestic, 10, 204, 206-8; as manager of the Michigan Theater, 24, 26, 30n9, 30n10, 38, 41, 49, 71, 82-83, 99, 203-4; photos of, 9, 89, 72, 91, 205, 206; retirement of, 92-93, 212; and Fred Waring, 10, 42, 208-10
Hoag, Jean, 205, 212
Hoffman, Floyd, 24, 216
Hogarth Management, 178
Holbrook, Hal, 139, 161
Holiday Inn, 59, 78n6
Holman, Woody, 118, 132
Hope, Bob, 59
Hopkins, Eugene, 153n12
Horn Blows at Midnight, The, 59
Hornung, Gena, 103

Hornung, Norman, 103
Houghton, Dick, 97, 217
House of Wax, 69
Hover, Helga, 180
Howland, Bob, 39, 40, 46n2, 216
How to Murder a Rich Uncle, 75
Hoyt, Emerson, 113
Humber, Richard, 43
Hunt, Mary, 113
Hutchins, Henry, 14n7

Iggy Pop, 121
Illuminata, 174
In a Chinese Temple Garden, 39
Intolerance, 160
Irish Rovers, 129, 136n3
Irwin, James R., 186-87
It Came From Outer Space, 69
It Happens Every Spring, 61
Ito, Robert, 67

Jackson, Joe, 188
James, Dennis, 101, 123, 143-44, 160
Jazz Singer, The, 37
Jenkins, Gordon, 102-3
Jewish Film Festival, 195
Johnny Belinda, 59
Johnson, Robert L., 118, 122, 134
Johnson, Van, 205
Jolson, Al, 37
Joseph Burstyn Inc. v. Wilson, 79

Kahn, Albert, 19
Kaplan, Wilfred, 113
Kass, Larry, 218
Keith, B. F., 15n12
Kerasotes Theatres, 163-64, 178
Ketelby, Albert W., 39
Key Largo, 59
King's Row, 59
Klaw and Earlanger, 15n12
Klingelhofer, Jan, 169, 181n2
KMD Foundation, 165

Korngold, Erich, 59, 186
Kresge Foundation, 171
Kronos Quartet, 157, 161

La Boheme, 160
Larsen, Lyn, 98-99, 101, 218
Lau, David, 97, 98, 103, 108n4, 113, 147, 199n1, 217
Lauter, John, 166n7, 199n1, 218, 219
Lawrence of Arabia, 164
Leaffe, Jim, 218, 219
League of Historic American Theaters, 197-98
Lean, David, 59
Leave Her to Heaven, 59
Lederer, Francis, 59
Legends of Rock and Roll, 188-89
Leibert, Dick, 199n1
LeLievre, Roger, 188
Leonard, Jim, 157
Levy, Ben, 98, 100, 102, 218
Lewis, Diana, 196
Lindbergh, Charles, 31n13, 38
Lipsky, Arie, 186
Littman-Peoples Theater (Detroit), 27
Loew's, 12
Logghe, Mike, 4, 14n7
Loring, Harold, 216
Lost Weekend, The, 59
Lotz, Richard L., 114, 119, 124n5
Love's Refrain, 6
Lucas, Clyde, 49
Lucas, Nick, 43
Ludmer-Gliebe, Susan, 156-57
Lunt, Alfred, 8
Lydia Mendelssohn Theater, 94n5

Madstone Theater, 192
Magnificent Ambersons, The, 59
Majestic Theater, 8-11, 15n12, 15n13, 26, 31n15, 42
Manos, Judy, 109n6
Mark Twain Tonight, 139, 141, 161
Mason, Sylvia, 67

Mass (Bernstein), 156-57, 166n2

"Masters of Movie Music," 186

Mayer, Lottie, 34

McCollum, John, 109n6, 153n16

McCoy, Clyde, 49

McKechnie, Donna, 185

McKinley Properties, 194

Mecouch, John, 146

Meet Me in St. Louis, 59

Meet the Michigan, 122, 123

Melbourne, Dale, 59

Menlove and Associates, 135

Mesler, Ray, 123, 127, 129, 132, 135, 136n3

Metro-Goldwyn-Mayer, 12

Michigan Community Theater Corporation (MCTC), 29, 114-15, 116-17, 124n4, 124n5, 125n9; board members of, 118; as owner of the Michigan Theater, 118-19

Michigan Theater: architecture of, 19-21, 26; attendance at, 121, 167n10; ballet at, 66-67; bands performing at, 43, 49; bond issue for, 120, 122; Broadway shows at, 141-43; change in ownership of, 118-23; changes during the 1960s, 81-86; Collins as executive director of, 139-40, 141-43, 144-45, 151, 161-62, 169, 179-80, 183, 198, 200n10; community support for, 112-23, 196; decline of, 87-92; during the Depression, 44-45; 50th anniversary of, 106-7; films shown at, 35-36, 45, 47n12, 59, 69-71, 83-84, 89-90, 108n3, 128, 151, 153n11, 163-64, 165, 167n15, 190; financial problems of, 134-35, 161-62; fire at, 131-32; first sound films at, 38-40, 47n12; fundraising efforts for, 133-35, 145-47, 169-71, 177; honored as Outstanding Historic Theatre, 197-98; independent films at,

194-95; lighting system at, 131-32; live presentations at, 22-23, 30n10, 33, 40, 41-42, 58-59, 61, 84-85, 94-95n8, 108n5, 121-22, 156, 157-58, 161, 185-88; marquee of, 20, 62, 110, 176-77; Mesler as manager of, 123, 127, 130, 133, 135; on the National Register of Historic Places, 100; opening night at, 22-26, 31n11; operating expenses of, 119, 124-25n6, 133; projection booth at, 22, 30n8, 38-39; remodeling of, 71-73; reopening of, 155-57; restoration of, 132, 136n5, 137n6, 147-51, 152n6, 170-71, 175-77; rock concerts at, 158-59; 75th anniversary of, 183; silent films at, 39, 98-99, 101, 106, 143-44, 160, 166n7, 187, 190; stage of, 21; and the State Theater, 179-80, 191-92, 193; strategic plan for, 191-94; and the Sundance Art House Project, 194-95; 3-D films at, 69-70; ticket prices at, 33; title transferred to, 193-94, 200n10; updating of, 132, 133, 136n5, 164, 195; ushers at, 57; vaudeville acts at, 34-35, 42-43; widescreen films at, 69. See also Barton pipe organ; Screening Room

Michigan Theater Foundation, 122, 123, 147; board of, 132-33, 213

Michigan Theatre (Jackson, Michigan), 27

Michigan Union Opera, 8, 41, 47n13, 61, 66

Michigenda, 8, 47n13

Mickey Mouse, 41

Milland, Ray, 61

Miller, Allen, 100

Miller, Arthur, 161

Miller, Barry, 95n17, 106, 118, 147

Miller, Jim, 218

Miller, Patsy Ruth, 24

Minick, John, 98

Minnelli, Vincente, 59, 73

Miracle, The, 79

Miramax, 165, 169, 181n1

Misch, Otto, 29

Monk, Meredith, 157

Monsieur Verdoux, 59

Monteux, Claude, 66

Moorehouse, Hank, 128

Moran, Selby, 6

motion pictures: censorship of, 74-77, 79n10, 79n13; and changing industry practices, 83-84; early days of, 1-2; ratings system for, 82, 211; synchronized sound for, 36-38, 46n5; technological improvements in, 67-71

Motor City Theatre Organ Society, 97, 100, 101-2, 112, 115, 121, 130, 147, 217

movie palaces, 5-7, 17-18, 107; wartime shortages affecting, 54-57. See also Michigan Theater

Movies at Briarwood Mall, 88, 90

movie theaters: chains, 12-13; declining attendance at, 65-66, 82-84

Movietone, 38, 39, 46n4, 46n5

Mrs. Miniver, 59

Muchnick, Ronnie, 206

multiplexes, 88, 90, 178

Murnau, F. W., 38

My Darling Clementine, 59

National Ballet of Canada, 67

National Velvet, 59

Negro Ensemble Theater, 157

Nelson, Ozzie, 49

Nelson, Rick, 120, 121

New Yiddish Theater (Detroit), 27

newsreels, 34, 53

nickelodeons, 2-3

Night at the Opera, A, 122

Not Just for Kids Series, 166n5

Now, Voyager, 122

O'Brien, Tony, 123, 125n12

Olivera, Hector, 101

Olmsted Brothers, 18

Once Upon a Castle (Daugherty), 186-87, 199n3

O'Neal, Joe, 146

Orpheum Theater, 5, 6-7, 13, 66, 72

Oscar Night America Party, 195-96

Otto, Alice, 104

Otto, Rupert, 102-3, 104, 111, 112, 115, 217, 218, 220

Outstanding Historic Theatre Award, 197-98

Packard, James, 113

Pandora's Box, 190

Paramount Publix, 12, 13, 15n15

Peninsula Productions, 156, 166n2

People's Popular Family Theater, 2

Peters, Jean, 61

Peterson, Kurt, 199n2

Petiet, Thomas, 113

Phillips, Al, 109n6

Photophone, 46n5

Piano, The, 165

Pidgeon, Walter, 59

Pieper, Louisa, 113, 191

Pinocchio, 59

Pipedreams, 187, 199-200n5

Pirates of Penzance, The, 84

Plank, Marcus L., 211

Plummer, Christopher, 161

Police, The, 158

Polich-Swain, Deborah, 167n11

Polish Film Festival, 195

Potter, Christopher, 142, 161, 166n2, 174

Poulos, Angelo, 18-19, 28-29, 181n4

Poulos, Niki Michael, 29

Poulos, Thalia, 28, 29

Poulos family, 181n4; and the sale of the Michigan Theater, 111, 114-15, 116-17

Prism Productions, 158-59, 165, 166n6

Psycho, 84

Quinn, Michael, 153n12

Radio City Music Hall, 5

Rae theater, 6, 13

Raitt, Bonnie, 188

Reagan, Ronald, 59

Rector, Gail, 140

Reed, Donna, 70-71, 78n7

Reed, William R., 210-11

Regent Theater (Manhattan), 5

Reid, Kate, 85

Rennie, Robin, 121

Reser, Harry, 43

Reynolds, Albert, 4, 14n7

RKO, 12

Road to Morocco, 59

Robe, The, 68

Robeson, Paul, 59

Robin Hood, 144

Robinson, Roger, 86

rock concerts, 158-59

Rogers, Andrew, 218, 219

Rogers, Buddy, 49

Rogers, Ginger, 59

Rogers, Harry, 34

Rolph, Marti, 199n2

Rolston, Howard, 98

Rosenthal, I. E., 14n6

Rowan, Jean, 192, 194

Rumelhart, Judy, 106, 109n6, 113, 117, 147, 149, 151, 156, 169, 185, 188, 200n6

Rundgren, Todd, 188

Ruth, Peter "Madcat," 123

Sagal, Peter, 189

Sale, Chic, 13

Sandifur, Virginia, 199n2

St. Clair, Carl, 141, 153n9

St. Joseph Mercy Hospital: fundraisers for, 105-6, 117

Sankai Juku, 157

Santry, Henry, 34

Saturday's Hero, 70-71, 78n7

Savoie, Jon, 130

Schlimmer, Jacob, 4-5

Schmitt, Conrad, 153n14

Schnitzer, Robert C., 85, 94n7

Schwartz, William, 14n6

Screening Room, 171-75, 181n8, 187

Second City, 156

Serious Fun! Series, 157, 160, 161

Seward, Emily, 219

Shackman, Grace, 2, 13

Shaven, Buster, 34-35

Shaw, Robert, 42

Sheik, The, 98

She Wore a Yellow Ribbon, 59

Shiel, Martha, 199n2

Shindell, Rick, 218

Shirley, George, 199n2

Sicotte, Vern R., 95n14

Simmons, Jean, 68

Simon, Neil, 161

Singin' In the Rain, 155

Smith, Scott, 199n1, 218, 219

Smith, Shirley W., 61, 62

Smokler, Irving, 165, 170, 171

Sound of Music, The, 118

South Pacific, 139

Spellbound, 59

Sperlin, B. W., 178

Sperlin, Billie, 178

Stachler, Tom, 158, 166n6

Stahl, Rose, 15n16

Stanchfield, Alan, 6

Star Theater, 3-5

State Theater, 66, 163, 164, 165, 178; and the Michigan Theater, 179-80, 191-92, 193; design and construction of, 50-53; marquee of, 48; opening of, 50; widescreen films at, 68-69

Steamboat Willie, 41

Steiner, Gayle, 199-200n5

Stephan, Art, 166n7, 187

Stevens, Wystan, 113, 114

Strony, Walt, 106

Sullivan, Louis, 6

Sundance Art House Project, 194-95

Sunrise, 38

Sutton-Smith, Emily, 199n2

Swisher, John, 113, 114, 117, 119

Taylor, Elizabeth, 59

Teagarden, Jack, 61

television, advent of, 65

That's Entertainment, 116

theater organs, 40-41. See also Barton pipe organ

Theatorium, 2, 13

Thief of Bagdad, The, 160

Three Campbells, the, 14n2

3-D films, 69-70

Three Musketeers, The, 160

Tiboni, Joe, 177

Time of Desire, The, 75-77

Tompkins, Paul, 44, 49, 61, 62, 85, 93, 97, 216-17

Towsley, Harry, 135

Towsley, Judy. See Rumelhart, Judy

Towsley, Margaret D., 117, 135, 146, 147, 169

Towsley Foundation, 171, 181n6

Treasure of the Sierra Madre, 59

Tremaine, Paul, 35

Tryon, Glenn, 24

Turpin, Ben, 13

Twelvetrees, Helen, 38

Under the Christmas Mistletoe, 185, 199n1

United States v. Paramount Pictures, 65

University Musical Society, 140, 143, 177

University of Michigan, 194, 199n2; growth of, 18, 191; theatre program at, 85

Up!, 195

Valentine Girl, The, 7

Valentino, Rudolph, 98

Vandenburg, Arthur H., 209-10

Van Sickle, Jay, 45

Vaudette, 2, 13

vaudeville acts, 1-2, 3, 12-13, 17; at the Michigan Theater, 34-35, 42-43

Vaudeville '80/81, 128

Veloz and Yolanda, 60, 61

Vidor, King, 59

Vipond, Fred, 218

VistaVision, 69

Vitaphone, 37, 39, 46n5

von Stade, Frederica, 185

Wagner, Brent, 199n2

Wait, Wait Don't Tell Me, 189

Wang, David Henry, 161

Waring, Fred, 10, 42, 91, 208-10

Warner, H. B., 59

Warner, Stephen, 199n1, 219

Warner, W. A., 216

Warner Bros., 15n15, 37

Washtenaw Council of Churches, 76

Wayside Theater, 80, 87, 163, 164

Weary River, 39-40, 46-47n10

Weems, Ted, 43

Weiderhold, Karl, 21, 24, 47n16

Weights and Measures, 6

Weinstein, Bob, 165

Weinstein, Harvey, 165

Weiser, Ron, 170, 171, 181n3, 181n7

Well! Well!, 6

Welles, Orson, 59

Westenfeld, George, 38

White Christmas, 69, 78n6

Whitlark and Young, 14n2

Whitney, B. C., 8

Whitney Theater, 8-11, 13, 66

Who's Afraid of Virginia Woolf?, 85, 94n7

widescreen films, 67-69

Wiernik, Julie, 212

Wilder, Billy, 59

Williams, John, 186

Wills, Chill, 887

Wilson, Brian, 188

Wilson, Charles E., 210

Wilson, J. Roland, 113, 124n1

Wiltse, Louis, 87

World War II: newsreels during, 53; shortages during, 54-57

Wright, Searle, 101

Wuerth, J. Fred, 6

Wuerth Theater, 6, 13, 16, 38, 66, 72; organ at, 6, 7

Yassick, Greg, 128

Yost, Fielding, 207

Young, Karen, 121